By Jessica Seinfeld

Deceptively Delicious

Double Delicious

The Can't Cook Book

Food Swings

FOOD SWINGS

FOOD SWINGS

125+ RECIPES TO ENJOY YOUR LIFE OF
VIRTUE & VICE

Jessica Seinfeld
with Sara Quessenberry

BALLANTINE BOOKS
NEW YORK

Published in the United States by Ballantine Books, an imprint of Random House,
a division of Penguin Random House LLC, New York.

BALLANTINE and the HOUSE colophon are registered trademarks of Penguin
Random House LLC.

Hardback ISBN 978-1-101-96714-0
Ebook ISBN 978-1-101-96715-7

Printed in China on acid-free paper

randomhousebooks.com

246897531

First Edition

Case and interior design by Laura Palese

TO MY HUSBAND, JERRY,
whose food swings
keep me constantly
entertained

CONTENTS

Introduction

MANY OF US swing between what we want to eat and what we have to eat. We've all had that meal that starts with grilled fish and a piece of watercress . . . and eventually results in you plunging your face into a molten chocolate cake. I've been there.

If you love food, eating different things at different times definitely makes life more interesting. Sometimes we eat healthy, sometimes we indulge. We can eat totally clean for a while, then we go off the rails.

We make these choices based on how we're feeling, what we're doing, whom we're with. You've got your pizza pals, wingmen, and foodies. You've got fitness fanatics, who see bathroom scales whenever you suggest dessert.

Most of us move back and forth between want-to's and have-to's. Each morning, a voice in my head says, "Pancakes and maple syrup or chia seeds and a banana?" This type of debate continues throughout the day. I swing between being virtuous and giving in to vice. Virtue usually wins—but I'm also a big fan of vice.

Of course, everyone defines these poles differently. Each of us has our parameters. For example, my very healthy and fit friend Joe likes a cold sliced steak salad for lunch. It fills him up with the protein and the greens he wants to eat, and keeps him from inhaling cheesecake at the end of a meal. My friend Amy likes to cook her chicken

thighs with the skin on, because the juicier and crispier result is more palatable to her. Amy also prefers to eat chicken rather than red meat, so the chicken skin keeps her in her zone. Without a doubt, there are people who will not like that I put these recipes in the Virtue section. But I put them there because I know that satisfying meals keep many of us eating virtuously without feeling punished. So on that note, you will find a little bit of everything in this book—vegan, almost vegan, gluten-free, and dairy-free recipes, each of which is noted at the top of a recipe.

In *Food Swings,* I offer my personal approach: recipes that speak to different sides of my personality. One half of the book has recipes for everyday eating, the other half is for when you need to feel the wind in your hair.

Either way, the important thing is to end up feeling satisfied when the dishes finally land in the sink. The more we deprive our bodies of what they're craving, the more our bodies keep trying to compensate. The more energy we expend, the more we need foods that replenish. The desire to eat an entire chocolate cake after a long run is no coincidence; your body is just trying to protect itself. We can certainly make better choices than a chocolate cake, but the point is, if you eat smart, wholesome food as well as occasional treats, you can stay healthy and still enjoy your life. (By the way, if you do go the chocolate cake route, our recipe on page 236 will make your head cave in.)

Food swings are normal, as long as they don't swing too far out of control. I favor the relatively steady rhythm of a grandfather clock: eating a variety of wholesome foods, and allowing yourself some splurges without guilt.

This is the way I like to eat and the way I love to cook. Some nights, I make a simple poached fish with ample vegetables and sparkling water. Other nights, I go for chicken parmigiana, with pasta and wine. I suspect many of you seek a similar balance.

I also make a point of staying active. To me, moving your body daily is as essential as brushing your teeth. I try to exercise most days of the week, walk as much as possible, ride my bike to work, and take the stairs. This makes me feel entitled to eat freely between the covers of this book.

Life is short. My grandmother, who lived to age ninety-nine, ate tons of butter; had a cocktail, a glass of wine, and dessert every night; and walked everywhere in Manhattan. It's a good recipe for life: aim for virtue, accept some vice, and stay active.

People always say, "Have a happy and a healthy . . ."

Not easy to do both at the same time.

I don't insist you do things my way. In fact, I assume most people have already established their own habits. For foodies, there are certainly plenty of voices out there that are louder, bigger, and more qualified than mine.

I don't have multiple test kitchens or a team of people churning out recipes all day. I'm a home cook, who works slowly and methodically with one intrepid comrade, Sara Quessenberry. Finding a cooking partner—with more experience and different skills than my own—makes recipe development much more fun.

Working together over the years, Sara and I have both come to believe in simple recipes that get dinner on the table for family and friends in less than thirty minutes. We love many of the same foods, and together create recipes that we hope will appeal to experts as well as beginners. We use a few select ingredients to achieve maximum flavor at minimum cost.

So, now that you've entered my particular corner of the cooking planet, I hope you'll stay and explore. I don't pretend to have all the answers on how to eat or live. Like most people, I am just trying to find what works for me. My goal is simply to be helpful to those who share a low-key, high-quality approach to food.

As you will be able to tell from this book, I like a lot of different things—health food and junk food, simple food and sophisticated food. I love bread and dessert, but also steamed fish and vegetables. I pretty much love it all (well, except capers).

I hope you find in these pages food that makes you feel good as well as have a good time. And recipes you want to make again. The rest is up to you.

—Jessica

VIRTUE

*The enjoyable thing about
being virtuous is that you don't have
to come up with any excuses.
No mental work required.*

BREAKFAST

Silver Dollar Banana Pancakes 5

Quinoa Banana-Date Muffins 6

Quinoa Egg Bowl 9

Fluffy Goat Cheese and Arugula Omelet 10

Spinach and Eggs = Sp'Eggs 13

Asparagus Nests 14

Poached Egg, Avocado, Whole-Grain Toast 17

Morning Salad 18

Breakfast Glory Bowls 21

AMARANTH BOWL WITH RASPBERRIES,
WALNUTS, AND COCONUT 21

CHIA BOWL WITH PEACHES, BLUEBERRIES,
AND TOASTED ALMONDS 21

QUINOA BOWL WITH ALMOND BUTTER, STRAWBERRIES,
AND HEMP SEEDS 23

Breakfast Toasts 25

POMEGRANATE AND YOGURT ON
WASA CRACKER 25

AVOCADO AND CUCUMBER ON WHOLE-GRAIN
TOAST 25

TOMATO, FETA, AND EGG ON SESAME
BROILED PITA 25

NUT BUTTER, APPLE, AND HEMP SEEDS
ON PUMPERNICKEL 25

STRAWBERRY AND AVOCADO ON
WHOLE-GRAIN TOAST 25

BANANA, CASHEW, AND COCONUT SPREAD
ON WHOLE-GRAIN TOAST 25

Smoothies 26

KALE-PINEAPPLE SMOOTHIE 27

RED PEPPER–MANGO
SMOOTHIE 27

BLUEBERRY-COCONUT SMOOTHIE 27

KIWI-APPLE SMOOTHIE 27

SILVER DOLLAR BANANA PANCAKES

MAKES **ABOUT 48** SILVER DOLLAR-SIZE PANCAKES
ACTIVE TIME: **40 MIN** · TOTAL TIME: **40 MIN**

Pancakes are my favorite food. These are gluten-free (or not, if you use regular flour). If you are a pancake lover, waste no time and get involved with these.

- 3 large eggs
- 1½ cups ripe bananas (about 3)
- ½ cup milk of choice, such as almond, rice, or cow
- 1½ teaspoons pure vanilla extract
- ¾ cup brown rice flour
- 2 tablespoons coconut flour
- 1½ teaspoons baking powder
- 1 teaspoon ground cinnamon
- ⅛ teaspoon kosher salt

Coconut oil or unsalted butter

Maple syrup and blueberries, for serving

PREHEAT THE OVEN (with the oven rack in the middle) to 250°F.

In a blender, combine the eggs, bananas, milk, and vanilla and blend until smooth. Add the rice flour, coconut flour, baking powder, cinnamon, and salt and mix on low speed to combine.

Heat a large nonstick skillet or a griddle over medium-high heat to get it nice and hot, then reduce the heat to medium-low. For each batch of pancakes, melt 1 teaspoon coconut oil or butter and swirl to coat the bottom of the skillet. Scoop the batter (using 1 tablespoon per pancake) into the skillet, spacing the scoops 2 inches apart. Cook for 2 to 3 minutes, until the bubbles on the top start to pop and the undersides are golden brown. Flip the pancakes and cook for about 1 minute more, or until golden and puffed. Transfer to a platter and keep warm in the oven while you make the rest of the pancakes.

Serve with maple syrup and blueberries.

I never ever throw out spotty, brown bananas. I throw them whole into the freezer instead. This way I always have ripe bananas on hand. It's faster to thaw a frozen ripe banana than to watch a green one ripen.

QUINOA BANANA-DATE MUFFINS

MAKES **12 MUFFINS** · ACTIVE TIME: **20 MIN** · TOTAL TIME: **40 MIN**

To quote my friends, "These are insane." Just make them.

Nonstick vegetable oil cooking spray
1¼ cups cooked (and cooled) quinoa (see below)
1¼ cups almond meal/flour
¼ cup coconut flour
1 teaspoon baking soda
1½ teaspoons ground cinnamon
¼ teaspoon grated nutmeg
½ teaspoon kosher salt
1½ cups ripe bananas (about 3)
1 cup pitted dates, such as Medjool
2 large eggs
1 teaspoon pure vanilla extract
½ cup chopped walnuts

PREHEAT THE OVEN (with the oven rack in the middle) to 350°F. Spray a 12-cup muffin pan with cooking spray.

In a large bowl, whisk together the quinoa, almond meal, coconut flour, baking soda, cinnamon, nutmeg, and salt.

In a food processor, puree the bananas and dates until smooth. Add the eggs and vanilla and pulse a few times to combine. Scrape into the quinoa mixture and stir to combine. Stir in the walnuts.

Divide the batter among the muffin cups. Bake for 20 to 24 minutes, until just set in the middle and a toothpick inserted into the center of a muffin comes out with just a few moist crumbs attached. Place the pan on a wire cooling rack and let the muffins cool for 10 minutes before turning out.

HOW TO COOK QUINOA

In a medium saucepan, combine 1 cup quinoa with 2 cups water over medium-high heat and let come to a boil. Stir once, cover with a tight-fitting lid, and reduce the heat to medium-low. Cook for 12 to 15 minutes, until the water is absorbed. Remove from the heat and fluff with a fork. Let stand, covered, for 5 minutes more.

MAKES ABOUT 4 CUPS

QUINOA EGG BOWL

SERVES **2** · ACTIVE TIME: **10 MIN** · TOTAL TIME: **15 MIN**

I always make a big batch of quinoa for the week to use for breakfast, lunch, or dinner. I can never decide at which meal I like it best, so here is a little breakfast/lunch combination.

  1   tablespoon extra virgin olive oil
1½   cups cooked (and cooled) red quinoa (see page 6)
10   cherry or grape tomatoes, quartered
  ¼   English cucumber, cut into small pieces
  2   large eggs
  2   scallions (white and light-green parts), sliced
Pinch of kosher salt, cayenne pepper, and freshly ground black pepper

IN A MEDIUM SKILLET, heat the oil over medium heat. Add the quinoa and cook, stirring, for 2 to 3 minutes, until toasted and crisp. Divide into bowls. Stir in the tomatoes and cucumber.

For the eggs, fill a medium saucepan with ½ inch of water, place over medium-high heat, and let come to a boil. If you have a steamer basket, put the eggs in it and lower the basket into the pan. Otherwise, carefully add the eggs to the water. Lower the heat to medium-low so the water simmers gently and cover with a tight-fitting lid. Steam the eggs for 6 minutes. This will give you a soft yolk with a perfectly cooked white. Immediately crack each egg several times on the side of the sink and peel. You can pass the eggs under cold running water while you peel if they are too hot to handle.

Place each egg on top of the quinoa. Sprinkle with the scallions, salt, cayenne, and black pepper.

FLUFFY GOAT CHEESE *and* ARUGULA OMELET

SERVES **1** · ACTIVE TIME: **10 MIN** · TOTAL TIME: **10 MIN**

I don't really like omelets. But the goat cheese, arugula, and chives, and the fluffiness from the whipped egg whites in this recipe pulled me into the light.

2 large eggs

1 tablespoon whole or low-fat milk

⅛ teaspoon kosher salt

⅛ teaspoon freshly ground black pepper

2 teaspoons extra virgin olive oil

½ cup chopped fresh arugula

8 cherry or grape tomatoes, quartered

2 tablespoons crumbled goat cheese

6 fresh chives, plus more for serving

SEPARATE THE EGGS: Crack the whites into a medium bowl, and add the yolks to a small bowl. Add the milk, salt, and pepper to the yolks and beat with a fork to combine. Vigorously whisk the whites for about 1 minute, or until they are fluffy and hold their shape.

Using a silicone spatula, gently fold the yolk mixture into the whites.

In a medium skillet, heat the oil over medium-low heat. Pour the egg mixture into the skillet and spread to cover the bottom. Cook, untouched, for 2 to 3 minutes, until the underside is golden brown. Spread the arugula, tomatoes, and goat cheese over half of the omelet. Use scissors to snip the chives into small pieces over the omelet. Fold in half and let it cook for 2 minutes, then flip it to the other side and cook for about 1 minute more, or until the eggs are set in the middle. Snip a few more chives over the top and serve.

SPINACH *and* EGGS = SP'EGGS

SERVES **4** • ACTIVE TIME: **15 MIN** • TOTAL TIME: **30 MIN**

I put this spinach fritatta in the breakfast section, but really this is an easy meal any time of day.

- 2 tablespoons extra virgin olive oil
- 1 yellow onion, sliced
- ½ teaspoon kosher salt
- 1½ pounds frozen spinach
- 8 large eggs
- 3 tablespoons whole or low-fat milk
- ½ cup grated Parmesan cheese
- ¼ teaspoon freshly ground black pepper

PREHEAT THE OVEN (with the oven rack in the middle) to 350°F.

In a medium ovenproof skillet, heat the oil over medium heat. Add the onion and ¼ teaspoon of the salt and stir to coat. Cover tightly and cook, stirring occasionally, for 6 to 7 minutes, until the onion starts to soften and begins to turn brown. Remove the lid and continue to cook and stir for 3 to 4 minutes more, until golden brown.

Meanwhile, put the frozen spinach in a colander and run under hot water to thaw. Squeeze out all of the excess water.

Crack the eggs into a medium bowl. Add the milk, Parmesan, pepper, and the remaining ¼ teaspoon salt. Whisk together.

Stir the spinach into the onion to heat through. Remove from the heat. Add the egg mixture. Gently stir to evenly distribute the eggs. Bake for 15 to 18 minutes, until the eggs are set in the middle. Cut into wedges and serve.

ASPARAGUS NESTS

SERVES **4** • ACTIVE TIME: **15 MIN** • TOTAL TIME: **15 MIN**

When you use a vegetable peeler on asparagus, you are giving people the impression that you know what you are doing in the kitchen. Therefore, serve this for brunch with friends.

- 1 pound asparagus
- 2 tablespoons extra virgin olive oil
- 2 tablespoons fresh lemon juice
- ¼ teaspoon kosher salt, plus more to taste
- ⅛ teaspoon freshly ground black pepper, plus more to taste

Small hunk of Parmesan cheese

- 8 large eggs
- 12 fresh chives

SNAP OFF THE woody ends of the asparagus (1 to 2 inches) and discard. One at a time, lay an asparagus spear flat on a cutting board and use a vegetable peeler to make long, thin strips. Place the strips in a large bowl. Add the oil, lemon juice, salt, and pepper. Toss well. Use the vegetable peeler to shave off pieces of Parmesan (about ⅓ cup) right into the salad. Toss again. Divide among bowls and shape into nests.

For the eggs, fill a medium saucepan with ½ inch of water, place over medium-high heat, and let come to a boil. If you have a steamer basket, put the eggs in it and lower the basket into the pan. Otherwise, carefully add the eggs to the water. Lower the heat to medium-low so the water simmers gently and cover with a tight-fitting lid. Steam the eggs for 6 minutes. This will give you a soft yolk with a perfectly cooked white. Immediately crack each egg several times on the side of the sink and peel. You can pass the eggs under cold running water while you peel if they are too hot to handle.

Place the eggs in the nests. Use scissors to snip the chives into small pieces over the eggs and shave some more Parmesan over the tops as well. Sprinkle the eggs with salt and pepper to taste.

If you're not a fan of asparagus, try zucchini instead.

POACHED EGG, AVOCADO, WHOLE-GRAIN TOAST

SERVES **4** • ACTIVE TIME: **15 MIN** • TOTAL TIME: **15 MIN**

This is what I will request for my last breakfast before I slide into the electric chair.

- 4 slices whole-grain bread
- 1 beefsteak tomato, sliced
- 1 avocado, sliced (see note)
- ½ cup sprouts, such as radish or alfalfa
- 2 tablespoons extra virgin olive oil
- 2 teaspoons white wine vinegar
- 4 large eggs

Kosher or flaky sea salt, freshly ground black pepper, and crushed red pepper flakes

TOAST THE BREAD and divide among plates. Top each with slices of tomato and avocado. Add the sprouts and drizzle with the oil.

To poach the eggs, fill a medium saucepan three-quarters full with water. Place over high heat and let come to a boil. Reduce the heat to medium so the water simmers gently. Add the vinegar. Crack an egg into a small bowl. Hold the bowl just over the surface of the water and let the egg slide in. Repeat with the remaining eggs. Cook for 3 to 4 minutes, until the whites are set but the yolks are still soft. Use a slotted spoon to lift the eggs onto a paper towel–lined plate.

Lay an egg over each toast and sprinkle with salt, black pepper, and red pepper flakes to taste.

HOW TO SLICE AN AVOCADO

First cut it in half and remove the pit. Using the tip of a paring knife, carefully slice the avocado flesh without slicing through the skin. Use a spoon to scoop out the slices.

MORNING SALAD

SERVES **4** · ACTIVE TIME: **5 MIN** · TOTAL TIME: **5 MIN**

This is a late-fall seasonal celebration on a plate and always a big hit at my Sunday brunches. The Spiralizer is the new Play-Doh Fuzzy Pumper Barber & Beauty Shop from my youth (Google it).

½ cup sliced almonds

2 apples, such as McIntosh or Empire

2 pears, such as Bartlett

2 tablespoons fresh lemon juice

2 navel oranges

½ cup pomegranate seeds

2 tablespoons honey

Grated nutmeg

IN A SMALL SKILLET over medium heat, toast the almonds for 3 to 5 minutes, tossing occasionally, until golden brown.

Use a Spiralizer (or a box grater) to make thin ribbons out of the apples and pears. Put them in a serving bowl and toss with the lemon juice.

Grate the zest of one of the oranges and set aside. Using a serrated knife, cut away the peel and white pith from the oranges. Then cut the oranges into thin rounds and lay them over the apple-pear mixture. Add the pomegranate seeds and almonds. Drizzle with honey and top with the nutmeg and grated orange zest to taste.

I always spray my measuring spoon with nonstick vegetable oil cooking spray before I measure honey. The honey slides right out instead of sticking to the spoon.

BREAKFAST GLORY BOWLS

Bowls of glory are part of my daily existence. They allow me to be creative,
and virtuous in a way that also somehow feels indulgent. Get cozy with these. Fill your pantry
with the different ingredients, and they will become a way of life.

AMARANTH BOWL WITH RASPBERRIES, WALNUTS, AND COCONUT

Serves 1 • Active time: 5 min • Total time: 15 min

- ¼ cup amaranth
- 6 walnut halves
- ¼ cup raspberries
- 2 tablespoons unsweetened coconut flakes, toasted (or not)
- 1 teaspoon honey

Pinch of ground cinnamon

IN A SMALL saucepan, combine the amaranth with ¾ cup water over medium-high heat and let come to a boil. Cover with a tight-fitting lid and reduce the heat to low. Cook for about 20 minutes, or until the amaranth is tender and the water is absorbed.

Spoon the amaranth into a bowl and break the walnuts into pieces over the top. Add the raspberries and coconut. Drizzle with honey and sprinkle with cinnamon.

CHIA BOWL WITH PEACHES, BLUEBERRIES, AND TOASTED ALMONDS

Serves 1 • Active time: 5 min • Total time: 20 min

- 2 tablespoons chia seeds
- ¼ cup milk of choice, such as almond, rice, or cow, or water
- 2 tablespoons sliced almonds
- ½ peach, cut into small pieces
- 2 tablespoons blueberries

Grated nutmeg to taste

IN A SMALL bowl, stir together the chia seeds and milk. Let stand for 12 to 15 minutes, until the chia seeds soften and become puddinglike (give a stir about halfway through).

Meanwhile, in a small skillet over medium heat, toast the almonds for about 3 minutes, tossing occasionally, or until golden brown.

Top the chia seeds with the peach, blueberries, almonds, and nutmeg.

recipe continues

MOM

*Teaching me how to cook was one of the smartest things
my mother ever did. She didn't do it to give me an essential life skill or
to instill in me a love of food. She did it because she needed someone
who could help with dinner before she got home from work.*

Food at our house was always nutritious. And that made it unlike anyone else's in our middle-class neighborhood. Back in the 1970s and 80s, organic groceries and health-conscious eating were just starting to surface. My parents somehow managed to be ahead of the curve. I'll never forget the smell of those health food stores—an earthy combination of grass, soil, cheese, and wooden crates. Around that time, my parents also started doing yoga and my dad stopped eating meat. Unfortunately for me, tofu and brown rice stir-fry became a staple. Our family joined a food co-op; I panicked when my parents said that membership required us all to volunteer there. My two siblings and I had to stock shelves and sweep up quinoa—not something I was eager to do at age fourteen.

Our pantry looked nothing like those of my friends. I could never figure out why none of my friends would ever come over for dinner. Their food was the stuff of tempting television commercials—dinners from cans, meals served in partitioned foil trays, pies that came in boxes. Our peanut butter was freshly ground, our cereal was puffed rice in bags, and our eggs were brown.

My mom was certainly not going to let me eat school lunches of hash browns and hot dogs. Despite being a working mother on a budget, she insisted on packing our lunches every day. I eyed my classmates' lunches with envy, wishing I had a bologna sandwich on white (and Doritos) instead of my carved turkey on brown bread (with sprouts) and fruit.

As much as I craved colorful breakfast cereals, it was during these early years that my palate adapted to wholesome food. And while as a teenager I was painfully embarrassed about my family's healthy habits, I now count myself fortunate for having been steeped in them.

Now, here I am, trying to carry on that same health-conscious tradition with my own kids, amid the quicker crappy options that in some ways have grown even more seductive (Fruit Roll-Ups? I rest my case). Most of the time, my pantry succeeds in looking similar to the one from my childhood. It's no surprise my daughter asks plaintively, "Why does everything in our house have seeds in it?" But, I am also more flexible than my parents were about treats and occasional junk food. I believe in finding a balance between deprivation and going off the deep end. If I get hit by a bus tomorrow, I don't want to die not knowing what baklava is.

QUINOA BOWL WITH ALMOND BUTTER, STRAWBERRIES, AND HEMP SEEDS

Serves 1 • Active time: 5 min • Total time: 20 min

¾ cup cooked (hot or cold) quinoa (see page 6)

1 tablespoon almond butter

4 strawberries, sliced

2 teaspoons hulled hemp seed hearts

1 navel orange

Splash of milk of choice, such as almond, rice, or cow

SPOON THE QUINOA into a bowl and top with the almond butter, strawberries, and hemp seeds. Grate the orange zest over the top (as much as you like) and add a splash of milk.

BREAKFAST TOASTS

SERVES **1** · ACTIVE TIME: **5 MIN** · TOTAL TIME: **5 MIN**

Light, quick, feel-good breakfasts or snacks any time of day.

POMEGRANATE AND YOGURT ON WASA CRACKER

Spread 2 tablespoons Greek yogurt over a Wasa cracker. Top with fresh pomegranate seeds, pepitas (pumpkin seeds), and a drizzle of honey.

AVOCADO AND CUCUMBER ON WHOLE-GRAIN TOAST

Mash together ½ avocado, 1 teaspoon fresh lime juice, ⅛ teaspoon kosher salt, and ⅛ teaspoon freshly ground black pepper. Spread over whole-grain toast. Top with sliced cucumber, toasted sesame seeds, and a sprinkle of chili powder.

VEGAN · DAIRY-FREE

TOMATO, FETA, AND EGG ON SESAME BROILED PITA

Cut a whole-wheat pita in half and split open. Brush 2 teaspoons extra virgin olive oil over one of the cut sides. Sprinkle with ½ teaspoon sesame seeds. Broil for 2 minutes, or until crisp. Top with sliced tomato, sliced hard-boiled egg, and crumbled feta. Sprinkle with dried oregano.

NUT BUTTER, APPLE, AND HEMP SEEDS ON PUMPERNICKEL

Spread 2 tablespoons nut butter over pumpernickel toast. Top with sliced apple, hulled hemp seed hearts, and a sprinkle of cinnamon.

VEGAN · DAIRY-FREE

STRAWBERRY AND AVOCADO ON WHOLE-GRAIN TOAST

Mash together ½ avocado, 1 teaspoon fresh lemon juice, and ⅛ teaspoon kosher salt. Spread over whole-grain toast. Top with sliced strawberries.

VEGAN · DAIRY-FREE

BANANA, CASHEW, AND COCONUT SPREAD ON WHOLE-GRAIN TOAST

In a food processor, finely chop 10 raw cashews. Add ½ of a small banana, 2 tablespoons unsweetened coconut, and a pinch of grated nutmeg. Pulse together until creamy. Spread over whole-grain toast. Top with fresh berries, a little more coconut, and nutmeg.

VEGAN · DAIRY-FREE

SMOOTHIES

SERVES 1 • ACTIVE TIME: **5 MIN** • TOTAL TIME: **5 MIN**

When you've given up on chewing your food.

KALE-PINEAPPLE SMOOTHIE

½ banana

½ cup coconut yogurt or Greek yogurt

2 to 3 tablespoons water

½ cup frozen kale or spinach

¼ cup frozen pineapple pieces

2 teaspoons grated fresh ginger

2 teaspoons hulled hemp seed hearts

In a blender, first blend together the banana, yogurt, and 2 tablespoons of the water. Then blend in the kale, pineapple, ginger, and hemp seeds until smooth. Add the remaining tablespoon of water, if necessary, for the desired consistency.

VEGAN · GLUTEN-FREE · DAIRY-FREE

RED PEPPER–MANGO SMOOTHIE

1 orange, peeled and cut into chunks

1 red bell pepper, cut into 2-inch pieces

¼ cup frozen mango pieces

Pinch of cayenne pepper

In a blender, first blend the orange. Then blend in the bell pepper, mango, and cayenne until smooth.

VEGAN · GLUTEN-FREE · DAIRY-FREE

BLUEBERRY-COCONUT SMOOTHIE

½ cup almond milk

¾ cup frozen blueberries

2 tablespoons unsweetened shredded coconut

2 tablespoons raw cashews

6 fresh mint leaves

In a blender, first add the almond milk, then the blueberries and blend until smooth. Add the coconut, cashews, and mint and blend again until smooth.

VEGAN · GLUTEN-FREE · DAIRY-FREE

KIWI-APPLE SMOOTHIE

1 orange, peeled and cut into chunks

1 kiwi, peeled and halved

1 apple, cored and cut into chunks

¼ cup frozen spinach

In a blender, first blend the orange, then blend in the kiwi. Add the apple and spinach and blend until smooth.

VEGAN · GLUTEN-FREE · DAIRY-FREE

When it comes to smoothies, frozen fruit and greens make for easier prep and faster cleanup. For easier blending, put your liquids in first and then add your chunkier fruits and vegetables. If your smoothie is too thick, you can always add a bit of extra water at the end to help smooth things out.

MEALTIME

TANGY and SPICY CHICKEN and PEPPERS

SERVES **4** · ACTIVE TIME: **15 MIN** · TOTAL TIME: **40 MIN**

As much as my family complains that I make too much chicken for dinner, they don't when I make this meal. It is a favorite and on weekly rotation.

8	skin-on, bone-in chicken thighs (about 3 pounds total)
¾	teaspoon kosher salt
½	teaspoon freshly ground black pepper
1	tablespoon extra virgin olive oil
3	garlic cloves
5	mixed bell peppers (about 2 pounds)
¼	cup white wine vinegar
½	teaspoon dried oregano
¼	teaspoon crushed red pepper flakes

PAT THE CHICKEN DRY with paper towels and season both sides with ¼ teaspoon salt and ¼ teaspoon pepper.

In a large skillet, heat the oil over medium-high heat. Add the chicken, skin side down, and cook for 10 to 12 minutes, until the skin is golden brown and crisp. Flip the chicken and cook for 2 minutes more (be careful of splattering).

While the chicken cooks, chop the garlic and slice the bell peppers into ½-inch-thick strips.

When the chicken has finished cooking, use tongs to transfer it to a plate. Pour off all but 2 tablespoons of the fat from the skillet. Return the skillet to medium heat. Add the bell peppers and cook, stirring and scraping up the brown bits from the bottom of the skillet, for 3 to 4 minutes, until the peppers start to soften. Stir in the garlic and cook for 1 minute more.

Add the vinegar, oregano, red pepper flakes, and the remaining ½ teaspoon salt and ¼ teaspoon black pepper. Add ½ cup of water and let come to a boil. Nestle the chicken into the bell peppers and let everything simmer together for about 15 minutes, or until the chicken is cooked through (you can cut into the thickest part to make sure). Add up to ¼ cup water if the liquid cooks away before the chicken is done. Serve the chicken with the bell peppers and sauce.

LEMON-THYME MILK-BRAISED CHICKEN *with* SPINACH

SERVES **4** · ACTIVE TIME: **15 MIN** · TOTAL TIME: **45 MIN**

Imagine yourself taking a milk bath scented with lemon and thyme. Just think how tender and flavorful you would be.

- 4 skin-on, boneless chicken breasts (6 to 8 ounces each)
- ¾ teaspoon kosher salt, plus more to taste
- ½ teaspoon freshly ground black pepper, plus more to taste
- 1 tablespoon extra virgin olive oil
- 4 garlic cloves, smashed and peeled
- 1½ cups whole milk
- 8 fresh thyme sprigs
- 1 lemon
- 10 cups packed spinach leaves, stems removed
- ⅛ teaspoon grated nutmeg

If you prefer, you can use skinless chicken breasts instead.

PREHEAT THE OVEN (with the oven rack in the middle) to 350°F.

Pat the chicken dry with paper towels and season both sides with salt and pepper.

In a large Dutch oven or ovenproof pot, heat the oil over medium-high heat. Add the chicken, skin side down, and cook, untouched, for 10 to 12 minutes, until the skin is well browned. Flip the chicken and cook for 2 minutes more. Use tongs to transfer the chicken to a plate.

Add the garlic to the pot and cook, stirring, for 1 minute, or until golden brown. Add the milk and thyme sprigs. Using a vegetable peeler, peel wide strips of zest from the entire lemon and add to the pot.

Once the milk mixture begins to boil, add the chicken, skin side up (it should not be submerged). Transfer the pot to the oven and roast, uncovered, for about 25 minutes, or until the chicken is cooked through (you can cut into the thickest part to make sure).

Divide the chicken among plates. Place the pot on the stove over medium heat and simmer the sauce for 2 minutes, or until it thickens slightly. Discard the thyme sprigs. Add the spinach and cook, stirring, for 2 minutes, or until wilted. Stir in the nutmeg. Taste for salt and pepper; you may want to add a little more. Serve the spinach alongside the chicken.

MUSTARD-WORCESTERSHIRE ROASTED CHICKEN

SERVES **4** · ACTIVE TIME: **15 MIN** · TOTAL TIME: **1 HOUR 15 MIN**

A one-pot happy meal. The Dijon mustard and Worcestershire sauce rub caramelizes in the oven and forms this beautiful crust on the chicken and leaves it extra juicy inside. Meanwhile, your vegetables are roasting alongside.

- 1 pound medium carrots (about 8)
- 1 head of garlic
- 4 large shallots, peeled
- 24 fresh thyme sprigs
- 2 tablespoons plus 2 teaspoons extra virgin olive oil
- ¼ teaspoon kosher salt
- ½ teaspoon freshly ground black pepper
- 1 4-pound whole chicken
- 3 tablespoons Dijon mustard
- 1 tablespoon Worcestershire sauce

PREHEAT THE OVEN (with the oven rack in the middle) to 425°F.

Cut the carrots in half crosswise, then cut them in half lengthwise (quarter them if they are fat). Cut the head of garlic crosswise in half. Cut the shallots lengthwise in half. Put them all in a large roasting pan with 12 sprigs of the thyme. Drizzle with 2 tablespoons of the oil and sprinkle with the salt and ¼ teaspoon of the pepper. Toss together and spread into a single layer, making room in the middle for the chicken. Place the garlic halves cut side down.

Pat the chicken dry with paper towels. Place the chicken in the middle of the vegetables and stuff with the remaining 12 thyme sprigs. In a small bowl, combine the mustard, Worcestershire sauce, and the remaining 2 teaspoons oil. Spread evenly over the chicken and sprinkle with the remaining ¼ teaspoon pepper. If you have kitchen twine, tie the legs together. If you don't, don't worry about it.

Roast for 50 to 60 minutes, until an instant-read thermometer inserted into the thickest part of the leg reads 165°F and the juices run clear.

Carve the chicken and serve with the vegetables. Pluck out the roasted garlic cloves and spread over the chicken.

MOROCCAN-SPICED CHICKEN *with* ARUGULA *and* ALMONDS

SERVES **4** · ACTIVE TIME: **15 MIN** · TOTAL TIME: **55 MIN**

A favorite meal of Mr. Jerry Seinfeld. Must be the Sephardic spices.

- 3 garlic cloves, chopped
- 2 teaspoons ground cumin
- 1 teaspoon ground coriander
- 1 teaspoon paprika
- ¼ teaspoon ground cinnamon
- ¼ teaspoon cayenne pepper
- ¼ teaspoon freshly ground black pepper
- ¾ teaspoon kosher salt
- 1 tablespoon extra virgin olive oil, plus more for the arugula
- 1 4-pound whole chicken, cut up into 10 pieces (breasts halved)
- 8 cups arugula
- ½ cup chopped roasted almonds
- 1 lemon, cut into wedges

PREHEAT THE OVEN (with the oven rack in the middle) to 425°F.

In a small bowl, combine the garlic, cumin, coriander, paprika, cinnamon, cayenne, black pepper, salt, and oil.

Pat the chicken dry with paper towels and put on a rimmed sheet pan. Rub with the spice mixture to coat completely. Roast the chicken, skin side up, for 35 to 40 minutes, until cooked through (you can cut into it to make sure it's no longer pink).

Arrange the arugula on a platter and drizzle with a little oil. Top with the chicken and almonds. Serve with lemon wedges.

MOMENTS OF WEAKNESS

Working with food is a lot of fun, but it is also full of temptation.

It requires a level of discipline I do not innately possess. To keep myself from going rogue and snacking indiscriminately, I've developed a few safeguards that help keep me in line—at least, most of the day.

These measures aren't complicated or revolutionary. That's the point—they are just precautions I take, so that I stand a chance of sometimes making a good choice rather than always making a bad one.

My old habit was to open a cabinet and gravitate toward the potato chips or cookies—in large part because they were the first items that caught my eye. Now, rather than hit the pantry first, I head straight for the fridge, where I keep cut-up raw vegetables in an ice bath at the forefront, and at eye level. It is the first thing I see when I open the door. It's hard to opt for junk food after being confronted by crisp, fresh vegetables. To make them more enticing, I dip carrots in peanut butter, smear cream cheese on celery, and sprinkle salt on red and green bell peppers.

In the evenings, I make chia pudding so that in the morning—instead of pancakes and French toast—I have a healthy option awaiting me. I throw berries, nuts, and maple syrup on top of the pudding to make a satisfying, quick, nutritious breakfast. Large mason jars of chia pudding will store three to four no-fuss breakfasts. I also always keep hard-boiled eggs in my fridge for when I get hungry between meals. Again, the best way to counter potential moments of weakness is through preparation. Then you can be more selective about when to indulge, and feel good about giving yourself those treats.

As much as I hate it, exercise matters. I do always feel good after I've done it, so I've made physical activity part of my routine. I've learned to accept it as mandatory. I try to do something for one hour five days a week. I also ride my bike or walk all over New York City. The commute to and from my downtown office alone burns 500 calories. In addition, I try to take a twenty-minute walk after I eat, rather than just go lie on the sofa. After doing the dishes, my husband and I take our dogs outdoors (as much as I try to lure our kids along, they are suddenly interested in getting their homework done). So off we go around the block or to do a loop in Central Park.

For my colleague Sara and me, a twenty-minute power walk can provide a welcome break from testing meals and desserts all day—immediately changing our brains and bodies.

My favorite type of exercise is the one-hour walk-and-talk I take with a friend every Sunday. It allows me a solid weekly catch up with someone I love. While not enough to keep my jeans fitting comfortably, these walks give me something to look forward to, an antidote to the exercise itself. Or as my husband says, "Women like long hikes because they can think, 'At least I'm not getting any fatter.'"

If given the choice, I would eat bread, pasta, dessert, and wine all day, every day. As I have grown older, it is very obvious that I cannot eat that way without consequences. So the watchful measures I take enable me to enjoy the times when I raise my glass of cabernet, twist my fork in linguine, and just let go.

LEMON-PEPPER CHICKEN WINGS

SERVES **4** · ACTIVE TIME: **15 MIN** · TOTAL TIME: **55 MIN**

I am always trying to come up with new wing recipes to satisfy the relentless wing cravings in our house. My family usually prefers traditional Buffalo or BBQ wings. These are better: they are roasted, not fried, and have no sugar and minimal salt added.

1	tablespoon black peppercorns
2	lemons
1	teaspoon paprika
1	teaspoon kosher salt
1	tablespoon extra virgin olive oil
2½	to 3 pounds chicken wings

HOW TO ZEST CITRUS

When grating citrus zest, be sure to grate only the colorful skin. Stop grating when you reach the white part (the pith) because it is very bitter tasting.

PREHEAT THE OVEN (with the oven rack in the middle) to 425°F.

Pour the peppercorns onto a cutting board. Using the back of a small skillet's round edge, firmly press down to crack them. (Make sure they are all cracked before adding or you might break a tooth!) Add to a large bowl.

Grate the zest from the lemons and add to the bowl along with the paprika, salt, and oil.

Pat the chicken dry with paper towels. Add to the bowl and toss to coat in the spices.

Transfer the chicken to a rimmed sheet pan and arrange in a single layer. Cut the zested lemons in half and place, cut side down, among the chicken.

Roast until the chicken is cooked through and no longer pink (you can cut into a wing to make sure) and the skin is golden brown and crisp, 30 to 40 minutes. Squeeze the roasted lemons over the chicken.

PINEAPPLE CHICKEN STIR-FRY

SERVES **4** • ACTIVE TIME: **20 MIN** • TOTAL TIME: **20 MIN**

A streamlined approach to stir-fry; you don't have to cook everything separately.

2 tablespoons grated fresh ginger

3 tablespoons reduced-sodium soy sauce

2 tablespoons rice vinegar

1 to 2 teaspoons Sriracha hot sauce

2 tablespoons extra virgin olive oil

2 skinless, boneless chicken breasts (about 8 ounces each), thinly sliced crosswise

1 red bell pepper, sliced

2 cups small fresh pineapple pieces

1 bunch broccolini, trimmed and cut into florets

3 cups cooked brown rice, for serving (see note)

2 scallions (white and light-green parts), thinly sliced

1 lime, cut into wedges

IN A SMALL BOWL, combine the ginger, soy sauce, vinegar, and Sriracha.

Place all of your prepped ingredients near the stove because this dish goes quickly once you start cooking.

In a large skillet, heat 1 tablespoon of the oil over medium-high heat. When the oil shimmers, add the chicken in a single layer. Let cook, untouched, for 2 minutes, then stir and cook for 1 to 2 minutes more, until cooked through. Add 1 tablespoon of the sauce to the chicken and stir to coat. Transfer the chicken to a plate.

Return the skillet to medium heat and add the remaining 1 tablespoon oil. Add the bell pepper, pineapple, broccolini, and the remaining sauce and stir to coat. Cover tightly and cook for 3 to 5 minutes, stirring twice, until the broccolini is tender. Add the chicken back to the skillet to heat through.

Serve over brown rice and top with scallions and a squeeze of lime wedge.

HOW TO COOK BROWN RICE

In a medium saucepan, combine 1 cup brown rice with 2 cups water over medium-high heat and let come to a boil. Stir once, cover with a tight-fitting lid, and reduce the heat to low. Cook for 40 to 45 minutes, until the water is absorbed and the rice is tender. Remove from the heat, fluff with a fork, and let stand, covered, for 5 minutes more.

———— MAKES 3 CUPS ————

ORANGE CHICKEN *with* ROSEMARY *and* TOASTED GARLIC

SERVES **4** · ACTIVE TIME: **20 MIN** · TOTAL TIME: **20 MIN**

More chicken. I know. But it's simple and the toasted garlic is (hands to the sky).

- 4 skinless, boneless chicken breasts (6 to 8 ounces each)
- ½ teaspoon kosher salt, plus more to taste
- ¼ teaspoon freshly ground black pepper
- ½ cup flour, brown rice or all-purpose
- 1 teaspoon paprika
- 3 tablespoons extra virgin olive oil, plus more if necessary
- 4 garlic cloves, smashed and peeled
- 2 tablespoons fresh rosemary leaves
- ½ cup fresh orange juice
- ½ cup reduced-sodium chicken broth

PAT THE CHICKEN DRY with paper towels. Season both sides with the salt and pepper. On a large plate, combine the flour and paprika. Dredge the chicken in the seasoned flour, shaking off the excess, and place on a clean plate.

In a large skillet, heat the oil over medium heat. Using tongs, add the chicken, smooth side down, and cook for 5 to 7 minutes, until the undersides are golden brown. Flip the breasts over and cook for 5 to 7 minutes more, until browned and cooked through (you can cut into the fattest part to make sure it is no longer pink). Transfer to a clean plate or platter.

If all of the oil in the skillet has been absorbed, add 1 tablespoon more. Add the garlic and cook, stirring, for 1 to 2 minutes, until golden brown. Stir in the rosemary and let cook for 30 seconds. Now add the orange juice and chicken broth. Stir up the yummy brown bits that are stuck to the bottom of the skillet. Simmer for 3 to 4 minutes, until the sauce starts to thicken slightly. Taste for salt; you might have to add a pinch more. Spoon the sauce over the chicken.

CHICKEN SALAD
with CREAMY
BASIL DRESSING

SERVES **4** · ACTIVE TIME: **20 MIN** · TOTAL TIME: **35 MIN**

I used to pick watercress for my grandmother in her yard, and she would make us chicken salad watercress sandwiches on white bread. Those were the days when you could eat white bread without someone gasping in horror.

FOR THE SALAD

- 4 skinless, boneless chicken breasts (6 to 8 ounces each)
- ½ cup sliced almonds
- 1 bunch watercress, trimmed
- 1 avocado, quartered
- 6 fresh chives

FOR THE DRESSING

- 1 cup Greek yogurt
- 1 cup tightly packed fresh basil leaves
- 2 tablespoons extra virgin olive oil
- 1 tablespoon fresh lemon juice
- ¼ teaspoon kosher salt
- ⅛ teaspoon freshly ground black pepper

FOR THE SALAD, put the chicken in a medium saucepan and cover with cold water by 2 inches. Place over medium-high heat and let come to a boil. Then cover tightly and remove from the heat. Let stand, covered, for 15 minutes. Transfer the chicken to a plate to cool to room temperature, then refrigerate to cool completely.

In a small skillet over medium heat, toast the almonds for 3 to 5 minutes, tossing occasionally, until golden brown.

For the dressing, in a blender, combine the yogurt, basil, oil, lemon juice, salt, and pepper. Blend until creamy and smooth.

To assemble the salad, divide the watercress and avocado among four bowls. Shred the chicken and add to the bowls. Spoon the dressing over each salad and sprinkle with the almonds. Use scissors to snip the chives into small pieces over the salads.

OVEN "FRIED" CHICKEN

SERVES **4** • ACTIVE TIME: **20 MIN** • TOTAL TIME: **1 HOUR 40 MIN**

Going back to my old-school *Deceptively Delicious* roots, this recipe kills. A little sweet potato gives a small pop of nutrients while making the chicken moist and juicy.

- 1 small sweet potato
- Nonstick vegetable oil cooking spray
- ½ cup whole-wheat flour
- 3 large egg whites
- 1½ cups panko (Japanese-style) bread crumbs
- ½ teaspoon paprika
- ¼ teaspoon cayenne pepper
- ½ teaspoon kosher salt
- 2 tablespoons extra virgin olive oil
- 8 chicken drumsticks (about 2 pounds total)

PREHEAT THE OVEN (with the oven rack in the middle) to 400°F.

To make sweet potato puree, stab the potato with a fork a few times, then put on a rimmed sheet pan. Bake for about 40 minutes, or until very tender and soft when squeezed. Puree in a food processor or mash with a potato masher (you should get about ¾ cup).

Spray a wire cooling rack with cooking spray and place over a rimmed sheet pan (this helps to ensure crispy chicken all the way around).

Set up your breading station: Add the flour to a medium bowl. In another bowl, whisk together the egg whites and sweet potato puree. In a third bowl, combine the panko, paprika, cayenne, salt, and oil.

Working one at a time, dredge a drumstick in the flour, then dip into the puree mixture to coat completely. Shake off any excess before you roll it in the panko. Place on the prepared wire rack.

Bake for 30 to 40 minutes, until the bread crumbs are golden brown and the chicken is cooked through (you can cut into a piece of chicken to make sure it is no longer pink). I wrap the ends of the drumsticks in foil so you can pick them up to eat them when they are hot. It's less messy too.

CHARD-WRAPPED COD

SERVES **4** · ACTIVE TIME: **15 MIN** · TOTAL TIME: **35 MIN**

This could win the prize as the healthiest recipe in this book. Make it when you are really trying to grab the reins and go, "Whoa!"

4   large Swiss chard leaves

4   pieces cod fillet (each about 6 ounces and 1 inch thick)

8   fresh basil leaves

1   red bell pepper, very thinly sliced

½   fennel bulb, very thinly sliced

1   jalapeño pepper, very thinly sliced

2   tablespoons extra virgin olive oil

¼   teaspoon kosher salt

⅛   teaspoon freshly ground black pepper

1   lemon, cut into wedges

PREHEAT THE OVEN (with the oven rack in the middle) to 400°F. Line a rimmed sheet pan with parchment paper.

Cut off the stems from the chard leaves. Then, cut out the thick, stiff part of the stem that runs up into the leaves (you want the leaves to wrap easily around the fish without resistance).

Place each piece of fish on the lower third of each chard leaf. Dividing evenly, top with basil, bell pepper, fennel, and jalapeño. Drizzle with the oil and sprinkle with the salt and pepper. Wrap the chard around the fish with the seam side down. Bake for about 18 minutes, or until the fish flakes easily and is opaque throughout. Serve with lemon wedges.

Before you shop for fish, check out Monterey Bay Aquarium's Seafood Watch (they have a great app too) to help you choose. It's a guide to sustainable seafood that tells you if a specific fish is farmed or wild, where it's from, and what your best choice is, as well as what to avoid.

GINGER SALMON
with SESAME CUCUMBERS

SERVES **4** · ACTIVE TIME: **20 MIN** · TOTAL TIME: **35 MIN**

Broiling is my favorite way to cook salmon. The top gets a little charred while the inside cooks gently so you can't overcook it. Well, you can . . . but you won't if you read the simple instructions below.

1½   pounds skinless salmon fillet (about 1¼ inches thick)

⅓   cup reduced-sodium soy sauce

2   tablespoons honey

2   tablespoons fresh orange juice

1   tablespoon grated fresh ginger (about a 1-inch piece)

Sesame Cucumbers (recipe follows)

PUT THE WHOLE salmon fillet in a large ziptop plastic bag. In a small bowl, combine the soy sauce, honey, orange juice, and ginger. Reserve 3 tablespoons of the mixture and set aside. Pour the remaining mixture over the salmon. Squeeze out the air and seal the bag. Refrigerate for 15 minutes to let marinate (flip the salmon over halfway through so both sides marinate evenly).

Preheat the broiler (with the oven rack about 4 inches from the top). Line a rimmed sheet pan with aluminum foil.

Place the salmon on the prepared pan and discard the marinade. Broil for about 5 minutes, or until the top of the salmon begins to char. Pull the pan out and spoon half of the reserved soy mixture over the salmon. Broil for 1 minute. Add the remaining soy mixture and broil

for 1 minute more. The top should be nice and charred but not burned.

You can check for doneness by inserting the tip of a paring knife into the thickest part of the salmon. If the salmon flakes easily but still has a slightly darker orange center (medium-rare to medium), then it's done. If not, or if you like your salmon cooked more, then broil for 1 to 2 minutes more. Cut into 4 pieces and serve with the Sesame Cucumbers.

SESAME CUCUMBERS

Serves 4

1   tablespoon sesame seeds

1   English cucumber, thinly sliced

½   to 1 jalapeño pepper, seeded and thinly sliced into half-moons

2   tablespoons fresh lemon juice

1   tablespoon extra virgin olive oil

¼   teaspoon kosher salt

1   tablespoon chopped fresh dill

Put the sesame seeds in a small dry skillet over medium heat. Cook, tossing, for 2 to 3 minutes, until toasted. Let cool.

In a medium bowl, combine the cucumber, jalapeño, lemon juice, oil, and salt. Stir in the dill and sesame seeds.

COD *with* GARLICKY TOMATOES *and* POTATOES

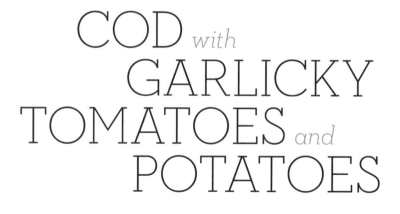

SERVES **4** · ACTIVE TIME: **20 MIN** · TOTAL TIME: **40 MIN**

A perfect weeknight meal. I make this at least once a week because somehow I have gotten my kids to love this too. It's probably the tomato-ey sauce.

- 2 tablespoons extra virgin olive oil
- 3 garlic cloves, smashed and peeled
- 1 pound baby potatoes (about 8), sliced into ¼-inch-thick rounds
- ½ cup dry white wine, such as pinot grigio
- 1 14-ounce can diced tomatoes
- ½ teaspoon smoked or regular paprika
- ¾ teaspoon kosher salt
- ¼ teaspoon freshly ground black pepper
- ¼ teaspoon crushed red pepper flakes
- 1½ pounds skinless cod fillet
- 1 lemon, quartered
- ¼ cup chopped fresh flat-leaf parsley

IN A LARGE SAUCEPAN, heat the oil over medium heat. Add the garlic and potatoes and cook, stirring often with a wooden spoon, for about 3 minutes, or until the garlic is golden brown. Add the white wine, tomatoes, paprika, ½ teaspoon of the salt, ⅛ teaspoon of the black pepper, and the red pepper flakes. Cover partially with a lid, reduce the heat to medium-low, and let simmer, stirring occasionally, for 15 to 20 minutes, until the potatoes are tender.

Season the fish with the remaining ¼ teaspoon salt and ⅛ teaspoon black pepper.

Place the fish on top of the potatoes and tomatoes, cover tightly, and let simmer for about 15 minutes, or until the fish flakes easily and is opaque throughout.

Squeeze the lemon over the fish and sprinkle with the parsley before serving.

PARSLEY PESTO STEAMED HALIBUT

SERVES **4** · ACTIVE TIME: **10 MIN** · TOTAL TIME: **20 MIN**

Break out your old steamer basket from the '80s for this recipe. Pesto makes this more intriguing for those who only moderately like fish.

- 1 garlic clove
- 1½ cups tightly packed fresh flat-leaf parsley
- ¼ cup pine nuts
- ¼ teaspoon kosher salt
- ⅛ teaspoon freshly ground black pepper
- 1 lemon
- ¼ cup extra virgin olive oil
- 4 pieces halibut fillet (each about 6 ounces and 1 inch thick)

FILL A LARGE POT with about 1 inch of water (or just enough to barely reach the bottom of the steamer basket when inserted).

Put the garlic, parsley, pine nuts, salt, and pepper in a food processor. Grate in the entire zest of the lemon. Pulse a few times until coarsely chopped. Add the oil and pulse a few more times until finely chopped (you don't want the pesto to be completely smooth).

Open your steamer basket and place the fish on it. Dividing evenly, spread the pesto over each piece of fish.

Turn the heat on to medium-high and let your pot of water come to a boil. Lower the steamer into the pot, cover tightly, and steam for 10 to 12 minutes, until the fish is opaque throughout and flakes easily with a fork. Cut the zested lemon into wedges and serve alongside the fish.

You can play around with pesto flavors here: swap out the parsley for fresh basil or cilantro.

WINE *and* GARLIC STEAMED MUSSELS

SERVES **4** · ACTIVE TIME: **15 MIN** · TOTAL TIME: **15 MIN**

This is the easiest, greatest, and cheapest recipe. The work is in cleaning the mussels, which really takes minimal effort.

48	mussels (see note)
2	tablespoons extra virgin olive oil
2	garlic cloves, chopped
¼	teaspoon crushed red pepper flakes
1¼	cups chopped fresh tomatoes
½	cup dry white wine, such as pinot grigio
¼	cup chopped fresh flat-leaf parsley

PUT THE MUSSELS in a colander. Put the colander in a large bowl in the sink and fill with cold water. Let the mussels soak a few minutes, then rub with your fingers to dislodge any dirt. If a long membrane (called a beard) is still attached, pull it off. Drain the mussels and throw away any that remain open.

In a large pot, heat the oil over medium heat. Add the garlic and red pepper flakes and cook, stirring, for 30 seconds until fragrant (you don't want the garlic to brown). Stir in the mussels and tomatoes, then add the white wine. Cook, covered with a tight-fitting lid, for 6 to 8 minutes, until the mussels open. Discard any that do not open.

Divide the mussels and broth into bowls and sprinkle with the parsley.

Store the mussels on a tray or in a bowl and cover them with a damp paper towel and refrigerate— never store in a sealed container. I like to cook them within 1 day of purchasing.

ROASTED BEEF TENDERLOIN *with* CHIMICHURRI

SERVES **4** • ACTIVE TIME: **30 MIN** • TOTAL TIME: **1 HOUR**

This is a Julian Seinfeld fave. Using Castelvetrano olives will immediately advance you into the genius category.

FOR THE TENDERLOIN

- 2 garlic cloves, chopped
- 1 tablespoon chopped fresh rosemary
- 2 tablespoons extra virgin olive oil
- 1½ pounds beef tenderloin
- ¾ teaspoon kosher salt
- ½ teaspoon freshly ground black pepper
- ½ cup grape tomatoes, halved
- ½ cup green olives
- ¼ cup fresh flat-leaf parsley

FOR THE CHIMICHURRI

- 1 small shallot
- 1 cup fresh flat-leaf parsley
- 5 tablespoons extra virgin olive oil
- 2 tablespoons red wine vinegar
- ½ teaspoon dried oregano
- ¼ teaspoon kosher salt
- ¼ teaspoon freshly ground black pepper
- ⅛ to ¼ teaspoon crushed red pepper flakes

FOR THE TENDERLOIN, in a small bowl, combine the garlic, rosemary, and 1 tablespoon of the oil. Rub all over the beef, put in a ziptop plastic bag, and let marinate in the refrigerator from 30 minutes to overnight.

Preheat the oven (with the oven rack in the middle) to 400°F. Let the beef come to room temperature (about 20 minutes).

In a large ovenproof skillet, heat the remaining 1 tablespoon oil over medium-high heat. Season the beef with the salt and pepper. Add it to the skillet and cook, turning occasionally, for 10 to 12 minutes, until well browned on all sides. Transfer the skillet to the oven and roast for 25 to 30 minutes, until an instant-read thermometer inserted into the thickest part reads 125° to 130°F (medium-rare). Let rest on a cutting board for about 10 minutes before slicing.

For the chimichurri, you can chop the shallot and parsley either by hand or in a food processor. Then combine in a small bowl with the oil, vinegar, oregano, salt, black pepper, and red pepper flakes.

Serve the tenderloin with the tomatoes, olives, parsley, and chimichurri.

STEAK SALAD
with SNAP PEAS, MUSHROOMS, *and* PARMESAN

SERVES **4** • ACTIVE TIME: **25 MIN** • TOTAL TIME: **45 MIN (PLUS COOLING TIME)**

Just the perfect meal.

FOR THE SALAD

- 1 pound sirloin steak (about 1 inch thick)
- 2 teaspoons extra virgin olive oil
- ½ teaspoon kosher salt
- ½ teaspoon freshly ground black pepper
- 8 cups chopped crisp lettuce, such as romaine
- ¼ cup chopped fresh chives
- 8 radishes, quartered
- 1½ cups sugar snap peas, halved
- ½ cucumber, sliced
- 8 button mushrooms, thinly sliced

Small hunk of Parmesan cheese

FOR THE VINAIGRETTE

- 1 tablespoon whole-grain mustard
- 2 tablespoons red wine vinegar
- ¼ cup extra virgin olive oil
- ¼ teaspoon kosher salt
- ¼ teaspoon freshly ground black pepper

LET THE STEAK come to room temperature (about 15 minutes).

In a medium skillet, heat the oil over medium heat. Sprinkle the steak with the salt and pepper. Add to the skillet and cook for 5 to 6 minutes per side, until an instant-read thermometer inserted into the center reads 125° to 130°F (medium-rare). Transfer to a plate and let cool to room temperature, then refrigerate to cool completely.

For the vinaigrette, in small bowl, whisk together the mustard, vinegar, oil, salt, and pepper.

To assemble the salad, in a large bowl, combine the lettuce, chives, radishes, snap peas, cucumbers, and mushrooms. Add the vinaigrette and toss. Divide the salad among plates. Slice the steak and add to the salads. Use a vegetable peeler to shave the Parmesan over the tops (as much as you like).

VEGGIE BURGERS
with PICKLED
CUCUMBER *and*
ONION

SERVES **4** · ACTIVE TIME: **35 MIN** · TOTAL TIME: **35 MIN**

I had given up on making veggie burgers at home until we came up with this.

FOR THE PICKLED CUCUMBER AND ONION

1 English cucumber, thinly sliced

¼ teaspoon kosher salt

½ red onion, thinly sliced into rings

3 tablespoons rice vinegar

2 teaspoons sugar

FOR THE BURGERS

1 15-ounce can chickpeas, drained and rinsed

2 tablespoons fresh lemon juice

2 tablespoons extra virgin olive oil

1 cup cooked (and cooled) quinoa (see page 6)

2 cups torn kale leaves

1 cup grated carrots (about 2 medium)

3 tablespoons sunflower seeds

1 teaspoon ground cumin

¼ teaspoon cayenne pepper (optional)

½ teaspoon kosher salt

4 whole-grain buns

8 butter lettuce leaves

FOR THE PICKLED cucumber and onion, in a medium bowl, sprinkle the cucumber with the salt and toss. Let stand for 10 minutes, or until the cucumber releases water. Squeeze out the water from the cucumber and discard any that has collected in the bowl. Add the red onion, vinegar, and sugar and toss. Set aside.

For the burgers, in a food processor, combine the chickpeas, lemon juice, and 1 tablespoon of the oil. Pulse several times until finely chopped. Add the quinoa, kale, carrots, sunflower seeds, cumin, cayenne, and salt. Pulse a few times until the mixture is finely chopped and everything is evenly distributed and holds together, but isn't completely smooth.

Divide the mixture into 4 even portions, then shape into ½-inch-thick patties.

In a nonstick skillet, heat the remaining 1 tablespoon oil over medium heat. Add the patties and cook until golden brown, 3 to 5 minutes per side. Be gentle when you flip as they are delicate.

Build your burgers with the buns, patties, lettuce, and pickled cucumber and onion.

QUINOA CHILI THAT IS NOT SILLY

SERVES **4 TO 6** · ACTIVE TIME: **20 MIN** · TOTAL TIME: **45 MIN**

Chili is one of the great food inventions. It works for a crowd, it works for the family, and this nourishing one works for everyone—vegans and meat lovers alike.

2   tablespoons extra virgin olive oil

1   yellow onion, chopped

4   garlic cloves, chopped

2   red bell peppers, cut into 1-inch pieces

2   medium sweet potatoes (about 1 pound total), peeled and cut into ½-inch pieces

2   tablespoons chili powder

2   teaspoons ground cumin

1   28-ounce can whole tomatoes

1   15-ounce can kidney beans, drained and rinsed

1   15-ounce can cannellini beans, drained and rinsed

1   tablespoon cider vinegar or red wine vinegar

1½ teaspoons kosher salt

¼   teaspoon freshly ground black pepper

½   cup quinoa

¼   cup chopped fresh flat-leaf parsley

IN A LARGE POT, heat the oil over medium heat. Add the onion and garlic and cook, stirring often, for 5 to 6 minutes, until softened.

Add the bell peppers and sweet potatoes to the pot and cook for 2 minutes. Add the chili powder and cumin and stir for 1 minute. Add the tomatoes and break them up with a spoon. Add the beans, vinegar, salt, pepper, and 2 cups water.

Turn up the heat to high and bring to a boil. Then reduce the heat to medium and simmer, stirring occasionally, for 10 minutes. Stir in the quinoa and simmer, stirring often, for about 15 minutes, or until the quinoa and sweet potatoes are tender. If the chili becomes too thick, you can add another ½ cup or so water. Stir in the parsley and serve.

DECEPTIVELY DELICIOUS TACOS

SERVES **4** · ACTIVE TIME: **20 MIN** · TOTAL TIME: **45 MIN**

My kids are not into beans. So, one night I had no meat or chicken but I had promised tacos. I mashed beans into salsa, and they had no idea. Now, for meatless taco nights I make these.

1   15-ounce can pinto beans, drained and rinsed
1½ cups cooked brown rice (see page 42)
¼   cup jarred salsa, plus more for serving
¼   teaspoon kosher salt
8   corn tortillas
1   cup grated Monterey Jack cheese
2   cups shredded romaine lettuce
½   cup sour cream
½   cup chopped red onion

IN A MEDIUM SAUCEPAN, heat the beans over medium heat. Add the rice and mash them together. Stir in the salsa and salt. Cover with a tight-fitting lid and keep warm over low heat.

Heat a dry large skillet or cast-iron skillet over medium-high heat. Add as many tortillas as you can so they fit in a single layer. Cook for 1 to 2 minutes per side, until speckled with toasty brown spots but still pliable. Keep warm in a clean dish towel. Repeat with the remaining tortillas.

Fill the tortillas with the bean mixture, Monterey Jack, lettuce, sour cream, red onion, and more salsa, if you like.

BAKED EGGS *with* TOMATOES, SPINACH, *and* PARMESAN

SERVES **2 TO 4** • ACTIVE TIME: **15 MIN** • TOTAL TIME: **25 MIN**

Clearly led by my DNA, I threw this together one night in a pinch. Come to find out it's an age-old recipe called shakshuka.

2 tablespoons extra virgin olive oil

2 garlic cloves, chopped

1 14-ounce can diced tomatoes

¼ teaspoon kosher salt

¼ teaspoon freshly ground black pepper

6 cups baby spinach leaves

4 large eggs

¼ cup grated Parmesan cheese

⅛ teaspoon crushed red pepper flakes (optional)

PREHEAT THE OVEN (with the oven rack in the middle) to 400°F.

In a medium ovenproof skillet, heat the oil over medium heat. Add the garlic and cook, stirring with a wooden spoon, for about 30 seconds, or until light golden brown.

Remove the skillet from the heat (to avoid splatters) and add the tomatoes, salt, and black pepper. Return to the heat and simmer for 8 to 10 minutes, until thickened. Stir the mixture occasionally as it cooks.

Now add the spinach to the sauce, cover with a lid, and let wilt for 1 minute. Remove the lid and stir in the spinach and cook for about 1 minute more, or until completely wilted.

Make a small well in the sauce with your spoon, then carefully crack an egg into it. Repeat with the remaining eggs. Sprinkle with the Parmesan and red pepper flakes, if you like some heat. Transfer to the oven and bake for 8 to 10 minutes, until the whites are set but the yolks are still soft.

EGGPLANT *and* CAULIFLOWER "MEATBALLS"

SERVES **4** · ACTIVE TIME: **30 MIN** · TOTAL TIME: **1 HOUR 25 MIN**

Even if you're a carnivore, you are going to be shocked by these vegetarian "meatballs."

- 1 eggplant (about 1½ pounds), peeled and cut into 1-inch cubes
- ½ head of cauliflower, cut into small florets (about 4 cups)
- 1 red bell pepper, cut into 1-inch pieces
- 4 garlic cloves, smashed and peeled
- ¼ cup extra virgin olive oil
- 1 teaspoon kosher salt
- ¼ teaspoon freshly ground black pepper
- ¼ teaspoon crushed red pepper flakes
- ½ cup farro
- ½ cup panko (Japanese-style) bread crumbs
- ½ cup grated Parmesan cheese, plus more for serving
- 2 recipes Marinara Sauce (recipe follows) or 5 cups of your favorite store-bought marinara

PREHEAT THE OVEN (with the oven rack in the middle) to 400°F. Line a rimmed sheet pan with parchment paper.

To another rimmed sheet pan or large baking dish, add the eggplant, cauliflower, bell pepper, and garlic. Drizzle with the oil and sprinkle with the salt, black pepper, and red pepper flakes. Toss together and arrange in a single layer. Roast for about 45 minutes, or until the vegetables are tender.

Meanwhile, cook the farro: Fill a medium saucepan with water and let come to a boil. Add the farro and cook for about 20 minutes, or until tender. Drain into a strainer and run under cold water to cool.

Put the roasted vegetables in a food processor and pulse until finely chopped but not smooth. Scrape into a large bowl and stir in the bread crumbs, Parmesan, and farro.

Shape the mixture into balls about 2 inches in diameter. Space them 1 inch apart on the prepared pan. Bake for about 20 minutes, or until slightly browned and crisp on the outside and heated through. Serve with the Marinara Sauce and a little more Parmesan.

MARINARA SAUCE

Makes about 2½ cups

2 tablespoons extra virgin olive oil
4 garlic cloves, thinly sliced
1 28-ounce can whole tomatoes
¾ teaspoon kosher salt
⅛ teaspoon freshly ground black pepper
¼ teaspoon crushed red pepper flakes

In a large skillet, heat the oil over medium heat. Add the garlic and cook, stirring often, for 2 to 3 minutes, until light golden brown. Add the tomatoes, salt, black pepper, and red pepper flakes. Break up the tomatoes with your spoon while the sauce simmers for 10 to 15 minutes, until slightly thickened.

A POT *of* BLACK BEANS

SERVES **4** · ACTIVE TIME: **10 MIN** · TOTAL TIME: **2½ HOURS**

For some reason making beans always seems daunting. But actually, the only work involved is waiting. Canned beans just can't compete, so give this a shot.

FOR THE BEANS

- 1 pound dried black beans (about 2¼ cups)
- 3 garlic cloves
- 1 dried bay leaf
- ¾ teaspoon ground cumin
- 1½ teaspoons kosher salt

FOR THE PICO DE GALLO

- 1 cup quartered cherry or grape tomatoes
- 2 tablespoons chopped red onion
- 2 tablespoons chopped fresh cilantro
- ½ jalapeño pepper, chopped
- 1 tablespoon fresh lime juice
- 1 tablespoon extra virgin olive oil

Pinch of kosher salt

POUR THE BEANS into a strainer or colander. Pick through the beans and discard any debris or pebbles. Rinse the beans.

Put the beans in a large pot and add 10 cups water (a 5:1 ratio water to beans). Smash and peel the garlic and add to the pot. Add the bay leaf and cumin. Place over high heat and let come to a boil. Put a lid on the pot, slightly askew, to partially cover. Reduce the heat to medium-low so the beans simmer gently.

Let the beans simmer for 2 to 2½ hours (maybe even 3, depending on their age), stirring occasionally, until the beans are tender but still hold their shape. Keep an eye on the pot while it simmers to make sure there is always enough water to keep the beans covered.

Once the beans are tender, stir in the salt. At this point, the cooking liquid should be more like a gravy (slightly thick). If the beans are still a bit soupy, turn up the heat and let the liquid cook down a bit to thicken.

For the pico de gallo, in a small bowl, combine the tomatoes, red onion, cilantro, jalapeño, lime juice, oil, and salt.

You can serve the beans right away (remove and discard the bay leaf first) or let them cool in their liquid and refrigerate them. I think they're even better the next day. Serve them topped with fresh pico de gallo.

QUINOA BOWL
with SPINACH, POMEGRANATE, *and* CHICKPEAS

SERVES **4** · ACTIVE TIME: **20 MIN** · TOTAL TIME: **20 MIN**

This is my favorite fall/winter lunch. Another plea to keep leftover quinoa in your fridge.

- 1 pomegranate
- 4 cups baby spinach leaves
- 4 cups cooked (and cooled) quinoa (see page 6)
- ½ English cucumber, sliced into half-moons
- 1 15-ounce can chickpeas, drained and rinsed
- 1 avocado, diced
- 4 tablespoons extra virgin olive oil
- 2 lemons, halved
- ½ teaspoon kosher salt
- ¼ teaspoon freshly ground black pepper

CUT THE POMEGRANATE in half. Hold one half over a large bowl and give the round side several whacks—the seeds should fall right out. You may have to open up the pomegranate to help release the hard-to-get seeds.

Divide the spinach and quinoa among bowls. Add the cucumber, chickpeas, avocado, and pomegranate seeds.

Drizzle 1 tablespoon of the oil over each salad, then give each salad a good squeeze of lemon. Sprinkle with the salt and pepper.

RICE NOODLE SALAD *with* CUCUMBER, PEANUTS, BASIL, *and* MINT

SERVES **4** · ACTIVE TIME: **20 MIN** · TOTAL TIME: **20 MIN**

Heavenly summer lunch. The crunch of the cabbage and peanuts makes me crazy.

FOR THE SALAD

- 6 ounces thin rice noodles (see note)
- ½ medium head of green cabbage
- ½ English cucumber, sliced into half-moons
- 1 red bell pepper, thinly sliced
- 4 scallions (white and green parts), sliced
- ¾ cup mix of fresh mint and basil leaves, torn
- ¾ cup chopped roasted peanuts

FOR THE VINAIGRETTE

- ¼ cup fresh lime juice (about 2 limes)
- 3 tablespoons toasted sesame oil
- 2 teaspoons Sriracha hot sauce
- ½ teaspoon kosher salt

FOR THE SALAD, place the noodles in a large bowl and cover with hot water. Let them soak for about 5 minutes, or until tender. Drain in a colander; shake out excess water.

Cut the cabbage half in half again through the core. Cut out the core and discard. As thinly as you can, slice the cabbage into fine shreds (about 8 cups total).

Divide the noodles, cabbage, cucumber, bell pepper, and scallions among bowls. Sprinkle the herbs and peanuts over the tops.

For the vinaigrette, in a small bowl, whisk together the lime juice, sesame oil, Sriracha, and salt. Drizzle over the salad.

Rice noodles can be found in the Asian section of your grocery store.

BROWN RICE BOWL
with BLACK BEANS, AVOCADO, *and* SWEET POTATO

SERVES **4** · ACTIVE TIME: **15 MIN** · TOTAL TIME: **55 MIN**

Cozy, cozy, cozy. And I always throw an extra sweet potato into the oven to have on hand for the week.

- 2 small sweet potatoes, unpeeled
- 3 cups cooked (warm or room temperature) brown rice (see page 42)
- 1 15-ounce can black beans, drained and rinsed
- 2 cups shredded romaine lettuce
- 1 avocado, sliced
- 1 cup salsa
- ¼ cup roasted pepitas (pumpkin seeds) (see note)

Pinch of chili powder

PREHEAT THE OVEN (with the oven rack in the middle) to 400°F.

Put the sweet potatoes on a rimmed sheet pan and bake for 35 to 40 minutes, until they are tender and can be easily pierced with a paring knife. Let cool before slicing into rounds.

Divide the rice, sweet potatoes, beans, lettuce, avocado, salsa, and pepitas among bowls. Sprinkle with chili powder.

Pepitas are a great snack, loaded with protein and lots of minerals like copper and magnesium. A small handful a day is just right.

CABBAGE BOWL
with CITRUS,
AVOCADO,
ALMONDS, *and*
COCONUT

SERVES **4** · ACTIVE TIME: **15 MIN** · TOTAL TIME: **15 MIN**

Crunchy cabbage makes me happy. Add in the rest of these ingredients, and I become euphoric.

FOR THE BOWL

- ½ cup sliced almonds
- 2 grapefruits
- 2 oranges
- 1 small head of green cabbage
- 2 avocados, sliced
- ½ cup unsweetened coconut flakes, toasted

FOR THE VINAIGRETTE

- ⅓ cup reserved orange and grapefruit juice
- 3 tablespoons extra virgin olive oil
- 2 teaspoons honey
- ¼ teaspoon kosher salt
- ¼ teaspoon freshly ground black pepper

FOR THE BOWL, in a small skillet over medium heat, toast the almonds for 3 to 5 minutes, tossing occasionally, until golden brown.

To section the citrus: Starting with a grapefruit, trim off both ends. Set it on one of its flat ends. Working your way around the grapefruit, use your knife to cut away portions of the peel and white pith, exposing the bright flesh. To cut out the sections, hold the grapefruit over a bowl and cut along a membrane toward the center. Do the same along the adjacent membrane. The section will release and fall into the bowl. Repeat with the other sections. Squeeze out the juice from the membranes. Repeat the process with the other grapefruit and the oranges over the same bowl.

Cut the cabbage into quarters through the core. Cut out the core and discard. Slice the cabbage into fine shreds (about 8 cups).

Divide the cabbage among bowls. Arrange the citrus sections (reserving the juices) and avocado slices over the cabbage. Scatter the coconut and almonds over each salad.

For the vinaigrette, whisk together the juice, oil, honey, salt, and pepper and drizzle over the bowls.

FARRO BOWL
with SHAVED BROCCOLI
and PARMESAN

SERVES **4** • ACTIVE TIME: **15 MIN** • TOTAL TIME: **30 MIN**

Using a chef's knife, I shave raw broccoli stalks into thin coins and pretend they are chips. I also throw them into salad. So think twice before you throw away that delicious but often overlooked part of the broccoli.

FOR THE BOWL

1	cup farro
1	head of broccoli
	Small hunk of Parmesan cheese
6	radishes, halved and thinly sliced
¼	cup chopped fresh flat-leaf parsley
½	cup tightly packed basil leaves, torn

FOR THE VINAIGRETTE

¼	cup fresh lemon juice
¼	cup extra virgin olive oil
¾	teaspoon kosher salt
¼	teaspoon freshly ground black pepper

FOR THE BOWL, fill a medium saucepan with water and let come to a boil. Add the farro and cook for about 20 minutes, or until tender. Drain in a strainer and pass under cold running water to cool. Shake out the excess water and put the farro in a large bowl.

Using a chef's knife, cut off and discard the bottom 2 inches of the broccoli stalk. Thinly slice the remaining part of the stalk and chop the head of the broccoli into small pieces. Add to the bowl.

Use the tip of a paring knife to break off small pieces of Parmesan (about ⅓ cup). Add to the bowl.

Add the radishes, parsley, and basil.

For the vinaigrette, in a small bowl, whisk together the lemon juice, oil, salt, and pepper. Pour over the salad and toss.

Barley is a great substitution for farro.

LETTUCE CUPS *with* CHICKPEAS, CARROTS, RAISINS, *and* PEPITAS

SERVES **4** · ACTIVE TIME: **15 MIN** · TOTAL TIME: **15 MIN**

I've always thought that the huge popularity of sandwiches is because they're so easy to pick up and shove in your face. Here's a more elegant way . . .

FOR THE LETTUCE CUPS

- 2 cups grated carrots (about 4 medium)
- 2 scallions (white and light-green parts), thinly sliced
- 1/3 cup golden raisins
- 1 15-ounce can chickpeas, drained and rinsed
- 1 head of butter lettuce
- 1 cup Greek yogurt
- 1/2 cup fresh mint leaves
- 1/3 cup roasted pepitas (pumpkin seeds)

FOR THE VINAIGRETTE

- 2 tablespoons fresh lemon juice
- 2 tablespoons extra virgin olive oil
- 3/4 teaspoon ground cumin
- 1/4 teaspoon kosher salt
- 1/4 teaspoon freshly ground black pepper

FOR THE LETTUCE CUPS, in a large bowl, combine the carrots, scallions, raisins, and chickpeas.

For the vinaigrette, in a small bowl, combine the lemon juice, oil, cumin, salt, and pepper. Drizzle over the salad and toss well.

To assemble the cups, separate the lettuce leaves and spoon the salad into each of them. Add a small dollop of yogurt to each and sprinkle with the mint leaves and pepitas.

VEGETABLE SOUP

SERVES **4** · ACTIVE TIME: **40 MIN** · TOTAL TIME: **40 MIN**

This is a great weekend project. I like to leave this on the stove all afternoon long on a Saturday or Sunday so people can help themselves whenever they want. And since there's no meat involved, it can sit out at room temperature without any worries.

- 3 tablespoons extra virgin olive oil
- 1 large yellow onion, chopped
- 1½ teaspoons kosher salt, plus more to taste
- 2 garlic cloves, chopped
- 2 celery ribs, cut into ½-inch pieces
- 2 medium carrots, cut into ¼-inch-thick half-moons
- 2 zucchini, cut into ½-inch pieces
- 4 ounces green beans, cut into 1-inch pieces (about 1 cup)
- 2 cups shredded savoy or green cabbage
- ¼ teaspoon freshly ground black pepper
- 1 15-ounce can kidney beans, drained and rinsed
- ¼ cup chopped fresh flat-leaf parsley
- ½ cup grated Parmesan cheese

IN A LARGE POT, heat the oil over medium-high heat. Add the onion and ½ teaspoon of the salt and cook, stirring often, for 5 to 6 minutes, until softened.

Add the garlic, celery, and carrots and cook, stirring often, for 3 to 4 minutes, until they start to soften.

Add the zucchini, green beans, and cabbage to the pot. Pour in 5 cups water and season with pepper and the remaining 1 teaspoon salt. Let come to a boil, then reduce the heat to medium and simmer for 10 to 15 minutes, until the vegetables are tender.

Stir in the kidney beans and parsley and simmer for a few minutes, until the beans are heated through. Taste for seasoning; you may want to add a little more salt. Serve topped with the Parmesan.

ROASTED CARROTS *and* CHICKPEAS *with* FETA VINAIGRETTE

SERVES **4** · ACTIVE TIME: **15 MIN** · TOTAL TIME: **55 MIN**

I don't know how to articulate my love for this dish/meal. It's an emotional thing.

FOR THE CARROTS AND CHICKPEAS

- 1   15-ounce can chickpeas, drained and rinsed
- 1½   pounds thin carrots (about 18)
- 2   tablespoons extra virgin olive oil
- 1   teaspoon ground cumin
- ½   teaspoon paprika
- ¼   teaspoon cayenne pepper
- ½   teaspoon kosher salt

FOR THE VINAIGRETTE

- 3   tablespoons fresh lemon juice
- ¼   teaspoon kosher salt
- ¼   teaspoon freshly ground black pepper
- 2   tablespoons extra virgin olive oil
- 2   scallions (white and light-green parts), sliced
- 3   tablespoons chopped fresh flat-leaf parsley
- ½   cup crumbled feta cheese

FOR THE CARROTS and chickpeas, preheat the oven (with the oven rack in the middle) to 425°F.

Pat the chickpeas dry with a paper towel. Pour onto a rimmed sheet pan. Add the carrots to the pan. Drizzle with the oil and toss to coat.

In a small bowl, combine the cumin, paprika, cayenne, and salt. Sprinkle over the carrots and chickpeas and toss again, then spread into an even layer.

Roast, giving the pan a shake about halfway through, for 35 to 40 minutes, until the carrots are tender.

For the vinaigrette, in a small bowl, whisk together the lemon juice, salt, pepper, and oil. Stir in the scallions, parsley, and feta.

Arrange the roasted carrots and chickpeas on a serving plate and spoon the vinaigrette over the top.

WHOLE ROASTED CAULIFLOWER, TOMATOES, and GARLIC

SERVES **4** · ACTIVE TIME: **10 MIN** · TOTAL TIME: **1 HOUR 5 MIN**

I love the drama of this whole roasted cauliflower—the presentation, the slicing—which always brings down the house.

2   pints cherry or grape tomatoes

4   garlic cloves, smashed and peeled

4   tablespoons extra virgin olive oil

½   teaspoon kosher salt

¼   teaspoon freshly ground black pepper

¼   teaspoon crushed red pepper flakes

1   medium head of cauliflower (about 2¼ pounds)

⅛   teaspoon paprika

¼   cup chopped fresh flat-leaf parsley

PREHEAT THE OVEN (with the oven rack in the middle) to 400°F.

Put the tomatoes and garlic in a large baking dish. Drizzle with 3 tablespoons of the oil and sprinkle with ¼ teaspoon of the salt, the black pepper, and red pepper flakes. Toss to coat.

Trim the large green leaves from the cauliflower and discard. Trim the stem so the cauliflower sits flat. Push the tomatoes aside and place the cauliflower in the middle of the dish. Drizzle the remaining 1 tablespoon oil over the cauliflower and rub to coat. Sprinkle with the paprika and the remaining ¼ teaspoon salt. Roast for about 1 hour, or until the cauliflower is tender and can easily be pierced with a paring knife.

Sprinkle the parsley over the cauliflower. Slice the cauliflower into wedges and serve with the tomatoes and garlic.

ROASTED SPAGHETTI SQUASH *with* ALMONDS, CINNAMON, *and* SAGE

SERVES **4** • ACTIVE TIME: **15 MIN** • TOTAL TIME: **1 HOUR**

This recipe checks all my favorite boxes: crunchy, savory, and sweet.

- 1 spaghetti squash (about 4 pounds)
- 1 tablespoon extra virgin olive oil
- 3 tablespoons unsalted butter
- 16 fresh sage leaves
- ½ cup sliced almonds
- ¼ cup raisins
- ½ teaspoon cinnamon
- ¼ teaspoon kosher salt
- ⅛ teaspoon freshly ground black pepper

PREHEAT THE OVEN (with the oven rack in the middle) to 400°F.

Using your chef's knife, cut the squash in half lengthwise and scoop out the seeds. Place the squash on a rimmed sheet pan and drizzle the oil over the flesh and rub to coat. Flip the halves over so they lie cut side down. Roast for 40 to 45 minutes, until they can be easily pierced with a paring knife.

Once the squash halves are done, remove them from the oven and let rest while you prepare the browned almond butter.

In a medium skillet, melt the butter over medium heat. Add the sage and cook, stirring, for 30 seconds. Now add the almonds and cook, stirring, until the almonds and butter start to brown, about 2 minutes (be careful the butter does not burn). Remove from the heat and stir in the raisins and cinnamon.

Flip the roasted squash halves over. Use one or two forks to shred the flesh into "spaghetti" strands. Scoop out the spaghetti and place on a platter or plate. Sprinkle with the salt and pepper and pour the almond butter over the top.

KALE +
TABBOULEH =
KABBOULEH

SERVES **6** · ACTIVE TIME: **30 MIN** · TOTAL TIME: **30 MIN**

The exciting news about this salad is that you really get to hone your chopping skills. Try it with a dollop of Lemony Hummus (page 108).

½ cup bulgur wheat

4 cups chopped kale leaves

1 pint grape tomatoes, quartered

3 scallions (white and light-green parts), chopped

½ English cucumber, cut into small pieces

3 tablespoons fresh lemon juice (about 1 lemon)

2 tablespoons extra virgin olive oil

½ teaspoon kosher salt

¼ teaspoon freshly ground black pepper

PUT THE BULGUR in a medium bowl. Cover with hot water by ½ inch. Let soak for about 30 minutes, or until tender. Drain in a strainer and shake out all of the excess water.

In a large bowl, combine the kale, tomatoes, scallions, cucumber, and bulgur. Add the lemon juice, oil, salt, and pepper. Stir well to combine.

KALE *and* AVOCADO SALAD *with* ORANGE-SOY DRESSING

SERVES **4** · ACTIVE TIME: **15 MIN** · TOTAL TIME: **15 MIN**

Another kale salad to feed your virtuous soul.

FOR THE SALAD

- ½ cup sliced almonds
- 1 bunch kale, leaves torn into bite-size pieces (about 12 cups), stems discarded
- ½ small red onion, thinly sliced
- 1 avocado, diced
- 2 tablespoons hulled hemp seed hearts (see note)
- 1 navel orange

FOR THE VINAIGRETTE

- 3 tablespoons fresh orange juice
- 1 tablespoon reduced-sodium soy sauce
- 2 teaspoons toasted sesame oil
- ¼ teaspoon kosher salt

Hemp seeds are a great addition to any vegetarian's diet. Two tablespoons gives you 5 grams of protein, making the seeds a great alternative to animal protein. And they have lots of vitamin E and zinc. I add them to just about everything. I love Bob's Red Mill brand, which you can find in many grocery stores now or online. Store them in the refrigerator or freezer.

FOR THE SALAD, in a small skillet over medium heat, toast the almonds for 3 to 5 minutes, tossing occasionally, until golden brown. Let cool.

In a large bowl, combine the kale, red onion, avocado, hemp seed, and almonds.

To section the orange, first trim off both ends. Set it on one of its flat ends. Working your way around the orange, use your knife to cut away portions of the peel and white pith, exposing the bright flesh. To cut out the sections, hold the orange over the salad and cut along a membrane toward the center. Do the same along the adjacent membrane. The section will release and fall into the bowl. Repeat with the other sections.

For the vinaigrette, in a small bowl, whisk together the orange juice, soy sauce, sesame oil, and salt.

Drizzle the vinaigrette over the salad and toss until well coated.

SHAVED BRUSSELS SPROUT SALAD *with* HAZELNUTS *and* PARMESAN

SERVES **4** · ACTIVE TIME: **15 MIN** · TOTAL TIME: **20 MIN**

I think this is fancy enough to serve at a dinner party, but easy enough to eat every day for lunch.

FOR THE SALAD

- ¾ cup raw hazelnuts
- 1¼ pounds Brussels sprouts (18 to 20 medium)
- ½ red onion, thinly sliced

Small hunk of Parmesan cheese

FOR THE VINAIGRETTE

- ¼ cup fresh lemon juice (about 2 lemons)
- ¼ cup extra virgin olive oil
- ½ teaspoon kosher salt
- ¼ teaspoon freshly ground black pepper

PREHEAT THE OVEN (with the oven rack in the middle) to 350°F.

For the salad, spread the hazelnuts on a rimmed sheet pan and bake for about 15 minutes, or until lightly browned and the skins start to split. Pour the hot hazelnuts onto a clean dish towel, wrap up, and let cool. Now give them a good massage until most of the skins come off. Coarsely chop the hazelnuts.

As thinly as you can (or using the blade attachment on your food processor), slice the Brussels sprouts.

In a large bowl, combine the Brussels sprouts, red onion, and hazelnuts.

To crumble the Parmesan, use the tip of a paring knife or a fork and break off small pieces from the hunk of Parmesan (about ¾ cup). Add to the salad.

For the vinaigrette, in a small bowl, whisk together the lemon juice, oil, salt, and pepper. Drizzle over the salad and toss until well coated.

CAULIFLOWER SALAD *with* OLIVES *and* ALMONDS

SERVES **4** · ACTIVE TIME: **15 MIN** · TOTAL TIME: **15 MIN**

Serve this one with just about anything: Parsley Pesto Steamed Halibut (page 57), Roasted Beef Tenderloin with Chimichurri (page 61), or Orange Chicken with Rosemary and Toasted Garlic (page 45), to name a few dishes.

FOR THE SALAD

- ¾ cup sliced almonds
- 1 head of cauliflower
- ¼ cup chopped fresh flat-leaf parsley
- 3 scallions (white and green parts), sliced
- ½ cup chopped green olives, such as Castelvetrano
- 1 jalapeño pepper, seeded and sliced into half-moons

FOR THE VINAIGRETTE

- ¼ cup fresh lemon juice
- 3 tablespoons extra virgin olive oil
- 1 tablespoon honey
- ½ teaspoon kosher salt
- ¼ teaspoon freshly ground black pepper

FOR THE SALAD, in a small skillet over medium heat, toast the almonds for 3 to 5 minutes, tossing occasionally, until golden brown.

Cut the core out of the cauliflower and discard. Pull the cauliflower apart into large florets. Thinly slice the florets and add to a large bowl. Add the parsley, scallions, olives, jalapeño, and almonds.

For the vinaigrette, in a small bowl, whisk together the lemon juice, oil, honey, salt, and pepper. Drizzle over the salad and toss until well coated.

Cauliflower Salad with Olives
and Almonds (page 101)

Shaved Brussels Sprout
Salad with Hazelnuts and
Parmesan (page 100)

SEINSALAD

SERVES **4** · ACTIVE TIME: **15 MIN** · TOTAL TIME: **15 MIN**

This is our house salad, featuring each child's favorite veggie.

FOR THE VINAIGRETTE

- 1 shallot, chopped
- 2 tablespoons red wine vinegar
- 1 tablespoon fresh lemon juice
- 2 teaspoons Dijon mustard
- 6 tablespoons extra virgin olive oil
- ¼ teaspoon kosher salt
- ¼ teaspoon freshly ground black pepper

FOR THE SALAD

- 1 large head of romaine lettuce
- 2 carrots, cut into sticks
- ½ English cucumber, cut into spears
- 1 red bell pepper, cut into strips

FOR THE VINAIGRETTE, in a small bowl, whisk together the shallots, vinegar, lemon juice, mustard, oil, salt, and pepper.

For the salad, slice the head of romaine lengthwise down the middle, keeping the core intact. Then cut the lettuce crosswise into bite-size pieces (you should get about 8 cups). Discard the core.

In a large bowl, toss the lettuce with as much vinaigrette as you like. Divide among bowls, with the vegetables.

Store the extra vinaigrette in a jar and refrigerate. Shake it up before using. I usually double this recipe so I always have it on hand.

BAKED VEGETABLE CHIPS

I don't know if anyone fully understands the power of crunchy.
But they will when they make this.

BRUSSELS SPROUT CHIPS

Serves 2 to 4 • Active time: 10 min • Total time: 30 min

1½ pounds Brussels sprouts (22 to 24 medium)
  2 tablespoons extra virgin olive oil
  2 garlic cloves, chopped
½ teaspoon kosher salt
⅛ teaspoon freshly ground black pepper

PREHEAT THE OVEN (with the oven rack in the middle) to 425°F.

Using a paring knife, trim off the ends of the Brussels sprouts. Peel the leaves away and add to a rimmed sheet pan. You will have to keep trimming the stem as you get closer to the center to help release the leaves. Once you get to the small heart of the sprout and can no longer separate the leaves, just cut it in half and add to the pan.

Drizzle with the oil and add the garlic, salt, and pepper. Toss with your hands so all of the leaves are coated evenly. Spread in an even layer and roast for 18 to 20 minutes, until the leaves are crisp and the edges are browned.

SWEET POTATO CHIPS

Serves 2 to 4 • Active time: 10 min • Total time: 2 hours

  2 tablespoons extra virgin olive oil or coconut oil
  1 medium sweet potato (about 10 ounces), peeled
Kosher salt

PREHEAT THE OVEN (with two oven racks toward the center) to 250°F. If using coconut oil, melt the oil in a small skillet over medium heat.

Hold the sweet potato upright on your cutting board and use a vegetable peeler to make long, wide strips from the top to the bottom of the potato. Once the potato gets too small and awkward to hold, lay it flat while you peel.

Put the strips on a rimmed sheet pan. Drizzle with the oil and toss with your hands to coat well. All of the strips should be evenly coated; if they seem dry, add a little more oil. They should not be soggy.

Now divide the strips between two rimmed sheet pans and arrange in a single layer (a little overlapping is okay). Bake for 1½ to 2 hours, until crisp. Sprinkle with salt and serve.

FLAX CRACKERS
with LEMONY HUMMUS

SERVES **4 TO 6** · ACTIVE TIME: **10 MIN** · TOTAL TIME: **2 HOURS**

Never thought of making crackers before? This is the best little snack to satisfy that 4 p.m. craving for salty, fried potato chips. A breeze to make but slow to bake. Another victory for crunchiness.

¼ cup golden flaxseeds

¼ cup brown flaxseeds

¼ cup hulled hemp seed hearts

2 tablespoons sesame seeds

2 tablespoons tomato paste

1 teaspoon ground cumin

½ teaspoon chili powder

¼ teaspoon chipotle powder (if you like spice)

¼ teaspoon kosher salt

1 teaspoon extra virgin olive oil

Lemony Hummus (recipe follows)

PREHEAT THE OVEN (with the oven rack in the middle) to 250°F. Line an 18 x 13-inch rimmed sheet pan with parchment paper.

In a medium bowl, combine the golden flaxseeds and brown flaxseeds with ½ cup water. Let stand for 15 minutes, or until the seeds absorb all of the water and become gelatinous. Add the hemp seeds and sesame seeds to the flax and stir to combine.

These will last for up to 2 weeks in a ziptop plastic bag.

In a small bowl, combine the tomato paste, cumin, chili powder, chipotle powder, salt, and oil. Add to the seed mixture and stir to coat evenly.

Pour the mixture onto the prepared pan. Using the back of a spoon or a small offset metal spatula, spread the mixture out as thinly and as evenly as you can (it should almost cover the entire pan).

Bake for 1½ to 2 hours, until the cracker is crisp. Let cool completely. Break up into small crackers and serve with Lemony Hummus.

LEMONY HUMMUS

Makes about 1½ cups

1 15-ounce can chickpeas, drained and rinsed

1 small garlic clove

2 tablespoons fresh lemon juice

½ teaspoon kosher salt

1 teaspoon ground cumin

⅛ teaspoon cayenne pepper

3 tablespoons extra virgin olive oil

In a food processor, combine the chickpeas, garlic, lemon juice, salt, cumin, cayenne, and oil and process until smooth and creamy. If necessary, add 1 to 2 tablespoons warm water for the desired consistency.

DESSERT

PEANUT BUTTER-BANANA V'ICE CREAM

SERVES **2 TO 4** · ACTIVE TIME: **5 MIN** · TOTAL TIME: **2 HOURS**

No dairy. No eggs. Yet a flavor and texture everyone will love. As you can see, it even caught me a little by surprise.

- 4 very ripe bananas
- ¼ cup peanut butter (smooth or chunky)
- 1 tablespoon coconut oil
- ½ teaspoon ground cinnamon
- ¼ teaspoon grated nutmeg

Pinch of kosher salt

SLICE THE BANANAS into ¼-inch-thick rounds and put in a ziptop plastic bag. Lay the slices flat in a single layer in the freezer so the rounds freeze individually and not in a big clump. Freeze the bananas for at least 2 hours or overnight.

Place the frozen bananas, peanut butter, coconut oil, cinnamon, nutmeg, and salt in a food processor or blender and let sit for 2 or 3 minutes. Then puree until creamy and smooth.

If you like a frozen yogurt consistency, then serve it up. If you like a firmer ice cream experience, spoon it into a container and freeze for about an hour.

ROASTED PLUMS *with* HONEY *and* PISTACHIOS

SERVES **4** · ACTIVE TIME: **5 MIN** · TOTAL TIME: **20 MIN**

Plums add a little spring to your summer.

8 ripe plums, apricots, or peaches
1 tablespoon honey, plus more for serving
2 tablespoons chopped pistachios
¼ cup fresh mint leaves

PREHEAT THE OVEN (with the oven rack in the middle) to 400°F.

Cut the plums in half and remove the pits. Arrange the plum halves, cut side up, in a large baking dish. Drizzle them with the honey, then turn them over. Roast for about 15 minutes, or until they just start to soften.

To serve, flip them back over and drizzle them with a little more honey. Sprinkle with the pistachios and mint leaves.

Any stone fruit will work for this simple recipe. The key to your success is ripe summer fruit.

COCONUT MILK PANNA COTTA

SERVES **4** · ACTIVE TIME: **10 MIN** · TOTAL TIME: **10 MIN (PLUS COOLING TIME)**

Coconut milk turns this classic Italian dessert on its head. Three ingredients, super easy, and dairy-free. How else can I sell you on this?

1½   teaspoons gelatin (see note)
1   13.5 ounce can coconut milk
3   tablespoons maple syrup
1   orange
Fresh berries, for serving

It's important to sprinkle gelatin over cold, not hot, water so it dissolves evenly. And never boil anything containing gelatin, as this will make the gelatin lose its power.

PUT 2 TABLESPOONS of cold water into a small bowl and sprinkle with the gelatin. Let it sit for 5 minutes, or until the gelatin is completely softened.

Pour the coconut milk into a liquid measuring cup. Give it a quick whisk so it is no longer separated. Pour 1 cup of the milk into a small saucepan and add the maple syrup. Turn the heat on to medium, and heat the mixture until it is hot but not boiling. Remove from the heat and add the gelatin. Stir until the gelatin is dissolved, then stir in the remaining milk.

Pour the mixture into the liquid measuring cup then divide evenly into four 5- to 6-ounce cups or ramekins. Wrap each with plastic wrap. Refrigerate for about 4 hours, or until set, and up to 2 days.

To unmold, run a paring knife around the edges of the panna cotta. Then gently slide the tip of the knife along the bottom of the cup to release the suction. Invert the cup onto a plate and let the panna cotta slide out. Or you can serve them in their cups. Grate a little orange zest over the tops and serve with fresh berries.

PINEAPPLE *with* MOLASSES *and* LIME

SERVES **6** · ACTIVE TIME: **10 MIN** · TOTAL TIME: **10 MIN**

You have to trust me here. You won't believe the perfect combination of these three ingredients.

1 whole pineapple

2 tablespoons molasses, such as unsulfured or date

Grated zest from 2 limes

CUT OFF THE top and bottom from the pineapple. Then quarter the pineapple lengthwise and cut out the core from each. Cut each quarter away from the skin. Slice the pineapple flesh crosswise into bite-size pieces.

Drizzle the pineapple slices with the molasses and grate the lime zest over the top. Serve right in its skin.

To select a ripe pineapple, find one where the bottom half is golden yellow with a sweet pineapple aroma and is without soft spots. Fun fact: pineapples don't continue to ripen after they are picked.

GINGER YOGURT PARFAITS *with* BROWN SUGAR-BERRY COMPOTE

SERVES **4** · ACTIVE TIME: **15 MIN** · TOTAL TIME: **15 MIN (PLUS COOLING TIME)**

The ginger mixed in with the yogurt really takes this to another level. Together with the simple compote, you have an elegant dessert.

FOR THE COMPOTE

- 1 cup sliced strawberries
- 1 cup blueberries
- 1 cup raspberries
- 2 tablespoons dark brown sugar
- 1 tablespoon fresh lemon juice

FOR THE YOGURT

- 2 cups coconut yogurt or Greek yogurt
- 2 teaspoons grated fresh ginger

- ¼ cup chopped roasted almonds

FOR THE COMPOTE, in a medium saucepan, stir together the strawberries, blueberries, raspberries, brown sugar, and lemon juice over medium heat. After a minute or two the berries will start to release their juices. Simmer for about 10 minutes, or until the berries break down and the juices start to thicken (the compote will thicken more as it cools). Refrigerate until completely cool.

In a small bowl, combine the yogurt and ginger.

To assemble the parfaits, set out four small glasses. Spoon 1 tablespoon of the compote into the bottom of each glass, then layer in ¼ cup of the yogurt mixture. Repeat with another layer of compote and then yogurt. Spoon a final tablespoon of the compote on top and sprinkle with the almonds.

CHOCOLATE-POPCORN-ALMOND CLUSTERS

SERVES **8** · ACTIVE TIME: **15 MIN** · TOTAL TIME: **25 MIN**

What I make for movie night at our house when I want my family to like me. I even manage to get in some hemp seeds.

- 1 tablespoon extra virgin olive oil
- ½ cup popcorn kernels (10 cups popped)
- 1 cup sliced almonds
- ¾ cup bittersweet or semisweet chocolate chips
- 2 tablespoons hulled hemp seed hearts

Flaky sea salt or kosher salt

LINE TWO RIMMED sheet pans with parchment paper.

In a large pot, heat the oil over medium heat. Add the popcorn and cover tightly. When the popcorn starts to pop, shake the pot. Remove from the heat once it stops popping. Divide between the prepared pans.

In a small skillet over medium heat, toast the almonds for 3 to 5 minutes, tossing occasionally, until golden brown.

To melt the chocolate, fill a medium saucepan with 2 inches of water and bring to a low simmer over medium-low heat. Put the chocolate in a medium bowl and place over the simmering water (the bottom of the bowl should not touch the water). Stir until the chocolate is melted and smooth. Alternatively, you can melt the chocolate in the microwave—just be sure to do it in small time increments, stirring each time to ensure the chocolate doesn't burn.

Dividing evenly, pour the chocolate over the popcorn, then add the almonds. Use two large spoons to toss so the chocolate is evenly distributed. Sprinkle with the hemp seeds and salt. Refrigerate for 5 to 10 minutes, until the chocolate sets. I like to serve this in individual bowls.

BAKED APPLES

SERVES **4** · ACTIVE TIME: **10 MIN** · TOTAL TIME: **50 MIN**

I love how the apples puff up and become tender against the sweet crunch of the honeyed walnuts.

- ½ cup chopped walnuts
- 2 tablespoons rolled oats
- 2 tablespoons unsweetened shredded coconut
- 2 tablespoons extra virgin olive oil
- 2 tablespoons honey
- ½ teaspoon ground cinnamon
- ¼ teaspoon grated nutmeg
- 4 apples, such as Pink Lady, McIntosh, or Empire

PREHEAT THE OVEN (with the oven rack in the middle) to 375°F.

In a small bowl, combine the walnuts, oats, coconut, oil, 1 tablespoon of the honey, and the cinnamon and nutmeg.

Cut out the tops of the apples (as you would a pumpkin), then use a melon baller or spoon to scoop out the core. Fill each apple with the walnut mixture and put in a baking dish. Bake for 30 to 40 minutes, until the apples are soft and start to puff up.

Drizzle with the remaining 1 tablespoon honey before serving.

WATERMELON-MINT GRANITA

SERVES **4** · ACTIVE TIME: **10 MIN** · TOTAL TIME: **3 HOURS**

We are freaks for watermelon. In the summer, this is a very popular dessert at our house.

- 4 cups seedless watermelon chunks
- ¼ cup sugar
- 2 tablespoons fresh lemon juice
- 6 fresh mint leaves

PUT THE WATERMELON in a blender and puree (you should get about 3 cups of juice). Add the sugar, lemon juice, and mint. Blend until the mint is finely chopped. Skim off the foam from the top. Pour into an 8 x 8-inch metal baking pan and put in the freezer.

After about 45 minutes, the mixture will start to form ice crystals. Stir it to break up the crystals—it should be more like a slushie at this point. Freeze again, without stirring, for about 2 hours more, or until completely frozen. Use a fork to scrape the watermelon ice into fine shavings. Serve in cold glasses.

Try with cantaloupe, honeydew, or strawberries.

CHOCOLATE-CHERRY-COCONUT DROPS

MAKES **30 DROPS** · ACTIVE TIME: **20 MIN** · TOTAL TIME: **20 MIN**

I consider these a hybrid between a snack and a dessert.

- 2 cups pitted dates, such as Medjool or Deglet Noor
- 1 cup dried cherries
- ½ cup dark chocolate chips
- ¾ cup unsweetened shredded coconut
- ¼ cup almond butter
- 3 tablespoons coconut oil
- ¼ cup hulled hemp seed hearts
- ½ teaspoon grated nutmeg
- 2 cups puffed Kamut, puffed brown rice, or puffed quinoa

PUT THE DATES, cherries, and chocolate in a food processor and pulse several times until finely chopped. Add ½ cup of the shredded coconut, the almond butter, coconut oil, hemp seeds, and nutmeg and pulse several times to combine. Add the Kamut and pulse a few more times to break up the kernels and combine into the mix (they should still be visible).

Use the palms of your hands to first squeeze then roll into small, two-bite-size drops. Roll them in the remaining ¼ cup shredded coconut.

These will keep for up to a week in an airtight container.

CHEESE PLATE

One of my friends has gotten very fit as he has gotten older. He is in his fifties but looks better today than he did twenty years ago. He told me his most effective trick for enjoying meals while staying fit has been to substitute a cheese plate for a sugary dessert. He says it leaves him very satisfied and full, and he isn't skipping the fun part. I love this idea and have taken to it myself. I bet some experts might argue this is a better option than a sugar bomb at the end of a meal. But it's your life and you can decide what works for you. I feel comfortable recommending a cheese plate to you, if you promise to stick to quality cheeses and pay attention to the quantity you put in your mouth. An ounce or two of cheese at dessert is responsible and reasonable and makes for a rich, satisfying, and wholesome finale.

HERE ARE SOME combinations you might find at dessert time at our house:

- Fresh ricotta + a small spoonful of raspberry jam
- Goat cheese + dried cherries or a fresh fig + pistachios
- Manchego + dates or blueberry jam + Marcona almonds
- Parmigiano-Reggiano + sliced pear or tangerine + walnuts
- Aged Cheddar + sliced apple + walnuts
- Blue cheese + dried apricot or fresh grapes + pecans + a drizzle of honey

VICE

*Sometimes you just need to
feel the wind in your hair.*

BREAKFAST

CINNAMON BUNS

MAKES **15 CINNAMON BUNS** • ACTIVE TIME: **30 MIN** • TOTAL TIME: **3 HOURS 45 MIN**

You actually can make these. And they are worth the effort.

FOR THE DOUGH

½ cup (1 stick) unsalted butter, plus more for the pans

1 cup whole milk

4½ cups all-purpose flour, plus more for kneading

½ cup granulated sugar

1 ¼-ounce packet (about 2¼ teaspoons) active dry yeast

1½ teaspoons kosher salt

2 large eggs, beaten

Few drops of extra virgin olive oil for the bowl

FOR THE FILLING

½ cup (1 stick) unsalted butter

½ cup packed dark brown sugar

¼ cup granulated sugar

1 tablespoon ground cinnamon

½ teaspoon grated nutmeg

Pinch of kosher salt

FOR THE GLAZE

1 cup confectioners' sugar

2 tablespoons whole milk

1 teaspoon pure vanilla extract

FOR THE DOUGH, in a small saucepan, melt the butter over medium heat, then add the milk and heat it until it is warm but not hot. Pour into a large mixing bowl (or the bowl of a stand mixer).

In a medium bowl, whisk together the flour, granulated sugar, yeast, and salt. Add to the milk mixture. Using an electric mixer with the dough hook or paddle attachment on low speed, mix together. Add the eggs and mix

for about 3 minutes, or until the dough comes together. It should be soft and tacky to the touch but it shouldn't stick to your fingers. If it does, add a little more flour, up to ⅓ cup. Turn the dough onto a lightly floured surface and knead for about 2 minutes, or until the dough is smooth and round and springy like a baby's bottom. Place the dough in a lightly oiled bowl and cover with a dry dish towel. Let rise in a warm place in your kitchen for about 2 hours, or until it has nearly doubled in size.

Butter two round 9-inch cake pans or a 9 x 13-inch baking dish.

For the filling, in a small saucepan, melt the butter over medium heat. In a small bowl, combine the brown sugar, granulated sugar, cinnamon, nutmeg, and salt. Add the butter and stir to combine.

Punch down the dough. Turn it onto a lightly floured work surface and, using a rolling pin, roll out into a large rectangle about 11 by 15 inches and ½ inch thick. Spread the filling evenly over the dough rectangle. Starting from the long side that is closest to you, tightly roll up the dough into a log. Lift onto a cutting board and slice crosswise into about 1-inch-wide pinwheels.

Arrange the pinwheels in the prepared pans about ¼ inch apart and cover with plastic wrap. Let them rise for about 45 minutes. Or you can refrigerate at this point and let them rise overnight in the refrigerator—just let them come to room temperature before baking. They also freeze really well at this point.

Preheat the oven (with the oven rack in the middle) to 375°F. Bake the cinnamon buns for 20 to 25 minutes, until golden brown and the filling is bubbling.

Make the glaze: Whisk together the confectioners' sugar, milk, and vanilla. Let the buns cool for 10 minutes before glazing.

FLUFFY BUTTERMILK PANCAKES *with* ROASTED BERRY SYRUP

MAKES **24 PANCAKES** · ACTIVE TIME: **30 MIN** · TOTAL TIME: **30 MIN**

I wish I could sleep on a bed of these pancakes.

FOR THE PANCAKES

- 2 cups all-purpose flour
- 2 tablespoons granulated sugar
- 2 teaspoons baking powder
- ½ teaspoon baking soda
- ½ teaspoon kosher salt
- 2 large eggs
- 1½ cups buttermilk
- ½ cup whole milk
- 1 teaspoon pure vanilla extract
- 2 tablespoons (¼ stick) unsalted butter, plus more for the pan

Confectioners' sugar, sifted, for serving

FOR THE SYRUP

- 1 pint strawberries, quartered
- 1 cup mixed blackberries and blueberries
- ½ cup maple syrup

PREHEAT THE OVEN (with the oven rack in the middle) to 400°F.

For the pancakes, in a large bowl, whisk together the flour, granulated sugar, baking powder, baking soda, and salt.

In a medium bowl, whisk the eggs. Add the buttermilk, milk, and vanilla and whisk together. Add to the dry ingredients and whisk until just combined—a few lumps are okay.

Melt the butter in a large nonstick skillet or griddle over medium heat. Then pour the melted butter into the batter and whisk in.

Return the skillet to medium-high heat to get it nice and hot, then reduce the heat to medium-low. For each batch of pancakes, melt about ½ tablespoon of additional butter and swirl to coat the bottom of the skillet. Scoop the batter (using about 2 tablespoons per pancake) into the skillet, spacing the pancakes 2 inches apart. Cook for 2 to 3 minutes, until the bubbles on the top start to pop and the undersides are golden brown. Flip the pancakes and cook for about 1 minute more, or until golden and puffed. Transfer to a platter and cover with foil to keep warm while you make the rest of the pancakes.

For the syrup, in a medium baking dish, combine the strawberries, blackberries, blueberries, and maple syrup. Bake for 7 to 10 minutes, just until the berries start to release their juices.

Serve the pancakes topped with the syrup and confectioners' sugar.

STRAWBERRY BUCKLE MUFFINS

MAKES **12 MUFFINS** · ACTIVE TIME: **15 MIN** · TOTAL TIME: **40 MIN (PLUS COOLING TIME)**

I just love the pairing of the words "buckle" and "muffin" together. In this recipe, they create an unstoppable force that you may or may not want to be at the mercy of.

Nonstick vegetable oil cooking spray

FOR THE BUCKLE TOPPING

- 1 cup all-purpose flour
- ⅓ cup rolled oats
- ¼ cup granulated sugar
- ¼ cup packed dark brown sugar
- ½ teaspoon ground cinnamon
- ¼ teaspoon grated nutmeg
- ⅛ teaspoon kosher salt
- 6 tablespoons (¾ stick) unsalted butter, melted

FOR THE MUFFINS

- 1¼ cups all-purpose flour
- ¾ cup granulated sugar
- 1 teaspoon baking powder
- ¼ teaspoon baking soda
- ½ teaspoon kosher salt
- ½ cup (1 stick) unsalted butter, melted
- 2 large eggs, beaten
- ½ cup sour cream
- 1 teaspoon pure vanilla extract
- 1 cup sliced strawberries

PREHEAT THE OVEN (with the oven rack in the middle) to 350°F. Spray a 12-cup muffin pan with cooking spray or line with paper liners.

For the buckle topping, in a medium bowl, whisk together the flour, oats, granulated sugar, brown sugar, cinnamon, nutmeg, and salt. Add the butter and stir to combine into crumbs. Refrigerate while you make the muffins.

For the muffins, in a large bowl, whisk together the flour, granulated sugar, baking powder, baking soda, and salt. Add the melted butter and give a quick whisk. Then add the eggs, sour cream, and vanilla and whisk until just incorporated. Fold in the strawberries.

Dividing evenly, spoon the batter into the muffin cups. Crumble the buckle topping evenly over the tops. Bake for 20 to 24 minutes, until a toothpick inserted into the center of a muffin comes out with just a few moist crumbs attached. Place the pan on a wire cooling rack and let the muffins cool before turning them out.

To measure flour, use a spoon to scoop it into a measuring cup, piling on more than you need so that the cup is filled to its edges. Do not pack it in. Then level it off by running the straight edge of a knife across the top of the cup, sweeping the excess flour back into the canister.

OLIVE OIL CAKE

I love this moist cake. It works for any and all occasions.

Nonstick vegetable oil cooking spray

1⅔ cups all-purpose flour

1 teaspoon baking powder

½ teaspoon baking soda

½ teaspoon kosher salt

2 large eggs

1 cup granulated sugar

Grated zest of 1 lemon

1 cup extra virgin olive oil

½ cup Greek yogurt

Confectioners' sugar, sifted, for serving

PREHEAT THE OVEN (with the oven rack in the middle) to 350°F. Spray a 9-inch springform pan or regular 9-inch round cake pan with cooking spray.

In a medium bowl, whisk together the flour, baking powder, baking soda, and salt.

In a large bowl, whisk the eggs. Add the granulated sugar and lemon zest and whisk vigorously for 1 minute. Your biceps should ache as the egg turns a lighter yellow. Now slowly drizzle in the oil while you whisk. The oil should be completely incorporated. Whisk in the yogurt.

Add the dry ingredients to the wet ingredients. Whisk together until just combined (do not overmix). Scrape the batter into the prepared pan.

Bake for 32 to 36 minutes, until a toothpick inserted into the center of the cake comes out with just a few moist crumbs attached. Place the pan on a wire cooling rack and let the cake cool for 25 minutes. Remove the ring (or invert the cake onto the rack) and let cool completely. Dust with confectioners' sugar before serving.

This cake stays fresh and moist for at least 3 days. Perfect for weekend guests. Hopefully the cake will outlast the guests.

GRAND MARNIER OVEN-BAKED FRENCH TOAST

SERVES **4** • ACTIVE TIME: **10 MIN** • TOTAL TIME: **30 MIN**

This is standard issue at my house on Sunday mornings. Make with lots of Grand Marnier if the kids are running around too much. I'm kidding. Not really.

2 large eggs

1 cup half-and-half

½ cup whole milk

3 tablespoons Grand Marnier

1 teaspoon grated orange zest

⅛ teaspoon grated nutmeg

4 1-inch-thick slices French or Italian bread

2 tablespoons (¼ stick) unsalted butter

Maple syrup and fresh fruit, for serving

PREHEAT THE OVEN (with the oven rack in the middle) to 375°F.

In a baking dish large enough to hold the bread slices in a single layer, whisk the eggs. Then whisk in the half-and-half, milk, Grand Marnier, orange zest, and nutmeg. Add the bread and let it soak, turning halfway through, for 5 minutes.

In a large ovenproof skillet, melt the butter over medium heat. Add the soaked bread slices to the skillet, shaking off any extra batter before you do. Let the slices cook for 3 to 5 minutes, until the undersides are golden brown. Flip, cook for 1 minute more, then transfer to the oven. Bake for 15 to 20 minutes, until golden brown, puffed, and crisp around the edges. Serve with syrup and fresh fruit.

If you are doubling the recipe, cook the French toast in batches in the skillet, then transfer to a rimmed sheet pan to bake.

BERRY CLAFOUTI

SERVES **6** · ACTIVE TIME: **10 MIN** · TOTAL TIME: **1 HOUR**

The first time I had a cherry clafouti, it changed me as a person. Here is a version, if you're in the mood to see the face of God.

Unsalted butter, for the baking dish

½ cup plus 3 tablespoons sugar, plus more for the baking dish

4 cups mixed raspberries and blackberries

1¼ cups whole milk

3 large eggs

2 teaspoons pure vanilla extract

½ cup all-purpose flour

¼ cup almond meal/flour

½ teaspoon grated lemon zest

⅛ teaspoon kosher salt

PREHEAT THE OVEN (with the oven rack in the middle) to 350°F. Butter a 2-quart shallow baking dish. Sprinkle a little sugar in the dish and shake to coat the bottom and up the sides.

Arrange the berries in a single layer over the bottom of the dish.

In a blender, combine the milk, eggs, ½ cup of the sugar, the vanilla, flour, almond meal, lemon zest, and salt. Blend for 1 minute. Skim off the foam. Pour over the berries in the bottom of the dish and sprinkle with the remaining 3 tablespoons sugar.

Bake for 50 to 55 minutes, until puffed and a paring knife inserted into the center comes out clean. Serve warm.

CINNAMON SWIRL COFFEE CAKE

SERVES **12 TO 16** · ACTIVE TIME: **25 MIN** · TOTAL TIME: **1½ HOURS (PLUS COOLING TIME)**

A fun fact: the Seinfelds are obsessed with any combination of coffee, cake, and/or coffee cake.

Nonstick vegetable oil cooking spray

FOR THE SWIRL

- ¾ cup walnuts
- ⅓ cup packed dark brown sugar
- 2 teaspoons ground cinnamon
- ¾ teaspoon ground cardamom

FOR THE CAKE

- 3 cups all-purpose flour
- 1½ teaspoons baking powder
- 1½ teaspoons baking soda
- ¾ teaspoon kosher salt
- 1 cup (2 sticks) unsalted butter, at room temperature
- 2 cups granulated sugar
- 4 large eggs
- 2 teaspoons pure vanilla extract
- 1½ cups sour cream

Confectioners' sugar, for serving

PREHEAT THE OVEN (with the oven rack in the middle) to 350°F. Spray a Bundt pan with cooking spray.

For the swirl, spread the walnuts onto a rimmed sheet pan and bake for 10 to 12 minutes, until fragrant and crisp. When cool enough to handle, chop them.

In a small bowl, combine the brown sugar, cinnamon, cardamom, and walnuts. Set aside.

For the cake, in a medium bowl, whisk together the flour, baking powder, baking soda, and salt.

In a large bowl (or the bowl of a stand mixer), use an electric mixer on medium-high speed to beat the butter until creamy. Add the granulated sugar and beat for about 3 minutes, or until light and fluffy. Scrape down the sides of the bowl with a silicone spatula. Add the eggs, one at a time, beating in completely before the next addition and scraping down the sides of the bowl as necessary. Beat in the vanilla.

With the mixer on low speed, mix in half of the flour mixture. Now mix in all of the sour cream. Then mix in the remaining flour mixture until just combined (do not overmix).

Spoon a third of the batter evenly into the prepared pan and smooth the top. Sprinkle half of the swirl mixture over the batter. Repeat with another layer of batter and the remaining swirl mixture. Spoon in the remaining third of the batter and smooth the top.

Bake for 45 to 50 minutes, until a toothpick inserted into the center of the cake comes out with just a few moist crumbs attached. Place the pan on a wire cooling rack and let the cake cool for 25 minutes. Run a paring knife around the edges of the cake to loosen it from the pan. Turn the cake out onto a platter and let cool completely. Dust with confectioners' sugar before serving.

SKILLET-ROASTED POTATOES *and* TOMATOES *with* SUNNY-SIDE-UP EGGS

SERVES **4** · ACTIVE TIME: **15 MIN** · TOTAL TIME: **1 HOUR 10 MIN**

First you are parboiling then roasting the potatoes, which will give you the crispiest breakfast potatoes in our stratosphere.

- 8 small Yukon gold or red potatoes (about 1 pound)
- 1 pint cherry or grape tomatoes
- 2 garlic cloves, smashed and peeled
- ¼ cup plus 1 tablespoon extra virgin olive oil
- ½ teaspoon kosher salt, plus more to taste
- ¼ teaspoon freshly ground black pepper, plus more to taste
- 4 large eggs
- 1 tablespoon chopped fresh flat-leaf parsley

PUT THE POTATOES in a medium saucepan and cover with cold water by 2 inches. Place over medium-high heat and let come to a boil. Reduce the heat to medium and simmer for 15 to 18 minutes, until they can be easily pierced with a knife. Drain and run under cold water to cool.

Preheat the oven (with the oven rack in the middle) to 425°F.

Using the palm of your hand or a small plate, smash the potatoes semi-flat on a cutting board. Scoop them up with a spatula and place in a cast-iron or ovenproof skillet. Add the tomatoes and garlic. Drizzle with ¼ cup of the oil and sprinkle with the salt and pepper. Roast for 35 to 40 minutes, flipping the potatoes halfway through, until they are golden brown and crisp.

For the eggs, in a medium skillet, heat the remaining 1 tablespoon oil over medium heat. Crack the eggs into the skillet, spacing them apart as well as you can, and let cook for 3 to 4 minutes, until the whites are set but the yolks are still soft. Sprinkle with parsley and salt and pepper. Serve with the potatoes.

To save time, I like to parboil the potatoes in advance, usually the day before, and keep them in the fridge.

ITALIAN EGGS BENEDICT

SERVES **4** · ACTIVE TIME: **15 MIN** · TOTAL TIME: **15 MIN**

Crisping prosciutto so it's light and crackly, along with some garlic-rubbed toast, has put some people over the edge, in my experience.

- 8 ¾-inch-thick slices ciabatta bread or baguette
- 2 tablespoons extra virgin olive oil
- 1 garlic clove, smashed and peeled
- 8 very thin prosciutto slices
- 2 teaspoons white wine vinegar
- 8 large eggs

Small hunk of Parmesan cheese

Kosher salt and freshly ground black pepper

PREHEAT THE BROILER (with the oven rack about 4 inches from the top).

For the toasts, place the bread slices on a rimmed sheet pan and brush both sides with the oil. Broil until toasted, 1 to 2 minutes per side. Rub the garlic over the tops of the toasts.

To crisp the prosciutto, place a large skillet over medium heat. Cooking in two batches, add the prosciutto in a single layer. Cook for 1 to 2 minutes per side, until crisp (as you would bacon).

Divide the toasts among plates and top with the prosciutto.

To poach the eggs, fill a large saucepan three-quarters full with water. Place over high heat and let come to a boil. Reduce the heat to medium so the water simmers gently. Add the vinegar. Crack an egg into a small bowl. Hold the bowl just over the surface of the water and let the egg slide in. Repeat with the remaining eggs. Cook for 3 to 4 minutes, until the whites are set but the yolks are still soft. Use a slotted spoon to lift the eggs onto a paper towel–lined plate.

Place an egg on top of each toast and grate Parmesan over them, as much as you like. Sprinkle with salt and pepper to taste.

SWEET SWEET POTATO FRITTATA

SERVES **2 TO 4** · ACTIVE TIME: **5 MIN** · TOTAL TIME: **1 HOUR**

It's like French toast without the bread.

- ½ sweet potato
- 4 large eggs
- 1 tablespoon heavy cream
- 1 teaspoon pure vanilla extract
- ⅛ teaspoon kosher salt
- ½ tablespoon unsalted butter
- Ground cinnamon and sugar, for sprinkling
- Maple syrup, for drizzling

PREHEAT THE OVEN (with the oven rack in the middle) to 400°F. Stab the potato with a fork a few times and put it on a rimmed sheet pan. Bake for 35 to 40 minutes, until tender (but not mushy) and a paring knife slides easily through it. Let cool.

Lower the oven temperature to 350°F.

In a blender, combine the eggs, cream, vanilla, and salt. Blend for 1 minute.

Remove the skin from the sweet potato, then slice the potato into ½-inch-thick rounds (about 8).

Place a small skillet on the stove and turn the heat on to medium. Add the butter. Once the butter melts, swirl the skillet to coat the bottom and up the sides. Add the egg mixture and let it cook, undisturbed, for 1½ minutes.

Remove the skillet from the heat. Lay the sweet potato rounds in the eggs in a single layer. Transfer to the oven and bake for 12 to 15 minutes, until the eggs are set.

Run your knife or a small spatula around the edge of the frittata to loosen it from the skillet. You can invert it onto a plate or serve it straight out of the skillet. Sprinkle with cinnamon and sugar and drizzle with maple syrup. Slice and serve.

CRISPY CHORIZO RICE *with* CRISPY EGGS

SERVES **4** · ACTIVE TIME: **15 MIN** · TOTAL TIME: **15 MIN**

Another good use for leftover rice. Crisp it up with some smoky chorizo and top with a crispy fried egg.

1 8-inch piece Spanish (dry-cured) chorizo (about 4 ounces)

2 tablespoons extra virgin olive oil

3 cups cooked (and cooled) white rice (see note)

3 scallions (white and green parts), sliced, plus more for serving

4 large eggs

Kosher salt and freshly ground black pepper

HOW TO COOK WHITE RICE

Some people struggle with making white rice. Here's how to do it: In a medium saucepan, combine 1 cup white rice with 1³/₄ cups water over medium-high heat and let come to a boil. Stir once, cover with a tight-fitting lid, and reduce the heat to low. Cook for 18 minutes, or until the water is absorbed and the rice is tender. Remove from the heat and fluff with a fork. Let stand, covered, for 5 minutes more.

— MAKES 3 CUPS —

FOR THE CRISPY RICE, slice the chorizo lengthwise in half, then slice it crosswise into thin half-moons.

In a medium nonstick skillet, heat 1 tablespoon of the oil over medium heat. Add the chorizo and cook, stirring, for about 1 minute, or until the chorizo starts to brown. Stir in the rice and scallions and spread into an even layer. Let cook, untouched, for 7 to 8 minutes, until the underside is crisp.

To make the eggs, in another medium skillet, heat the remaining 1 tablespoon oil over medium heat. Crack the eggs into the skillet, spacing them apart as well as you can, and let cook for 3 to 5 minutes, until the whites are set and crisp around the edges.

Divide the rice among plates and top with the eggs. Sprinkle with some more scallions and season the eggs with salt and pepper.

GOAT CHEESE *and* DILL QUICHE

SERVES **6** · ACTIVE TIME: **30 MIN** · TOTAL TIME: **1 HOUR 30 MIN**

I would serve this breakfast, lunch, and dinner on a weekend, which usually happens when I make one.

FOR THE CRUST

- 1¼ cups all-purpose flour, plus more for the work surface
- ½ teaspoon kosher salt
- ½ cup (1 stick) cold unsalted butter, cut into small pieces

FOR THE FILLING

- 4 large eggs
- 1½ cups half-and-half
- ½ teaspoon kosher salt
- ⅛ teaspoon freshly ground black pepper
- 2 tablespoons chopped fresh dill
- 2 tablespoons chopped fresh chives
- 2 tablespoons chopped fresh flat-leaf parsley
- 6 ounces fresh goat cheese

PREHEAT THE OVEN (with the oven rack in the lowest position) to 375°F.

For the crust, in a food processor, combine the flour and salt. Add the butter and pulse several times in short, quick pulses until the butter pieces are pea-size. Then add 3 tablespoons ice water. Pulse a few times just to incorporate the water (you don't want to overmix). The dough should look like moist crumbs and hold together when pinched. If it's a bit dry and doesn't hold together, add another tablespoon of ice water and pulse twice.

Turn out the dough onto a lightly floured work surface. Gather up the crumbs and knead a few times until the dough comes together. Shape into a 1-inch-thick round disk.

Pressing evenly, roll the dough out into a large ¼-inch-thick circle, occasionally rotating it to help keep its round shape (sprinkle with a little more flour, both on top and underneath, if the dough starts to stick).

Lay the dough into a 9½-inch fluted tart pan with a removable bottom. Gently press the dough into the corners. Fold the overhanging dough back inside and press to seal (the top of the crust should be just a little higher than the pan). Refrigerate while you make the filling.

In a medium bowl, whisk together the eggs. Whisk in the half-and-half, salt, pepper, dill, chives, and parsley.

Set the tart pan on a rimmed sheet pan. Slice the goat cheese into ½-inch-thick rounds and arrange over the bottom of the crust. Pour in the filling. Bake for 50 to 60 minutes, until the filling is puffed and set in the middle and the crust is golden brown. Serve warm or at room temperature.

YOU COOK?

Oh, jeez: not another cookbook from an author of questionable skills.
And she's the wife of a celebrity?

I get it. You can roll your eyes.

Yes, I never went to cooking school. And no, I don't cook for a living. I have, however, been cooking since I was a kid. My mom worked and commuted long hours, so she always needed help getting dinner on the table. As the middle child of three, I had no choice but to interpret my mom's handwritten instructions and wing it until she got home.

I never had money to eat at restaurants in high school or college; I was too busy working at them anyway as a bus girl, waitress, salad assembler, or dessert maker. I also worked at the local Sheraton hotel, catering weddings and parties. For a student helping to pay her tuition, the free staff meals were a boon. And when I wasn't working, the last thing I wanted to do was go sit in another restaurant, and eat restaurant food. So, while my friends ate out and complained about being broke, I cooked for myself and saved a lot of money. I learned then how much better food tastes when you make it yourself, and how much money you save when you do. So, a few years later, when I met my now husband, one of the first things he said to me, incredulously, was, "You COOK?" That was his response when he asked me out to dinner for our first date and I answered that I would prefer to cook for him. I've been doing just that for the last eighteen years.

Yes, cooking takes some skill, confidence, and time. I wrote *The Can't Cook Book* for those who lack one or all of those things. I'll sum it up for you here: the key lies in being organized—meal planning, shopping, and reading the recipe ahead of time so you know what comes next.

While I generally find cooking relaxing and creative, I also know that having to make dinner after a long day of work, shuttling kids, and meal prep can definitely dampen the fun. But families need to eat every night, so I have found ways to make this daily requirement more tolerable, and even slightly enjoyable.

I've established a routine: select five recipes for the week, print them out on Saturday, shop sometime over the weekend (while my husband waits in the car), and pick up fresh items as needed during the week. Most important, I have learned to better anticipate the whole enterprise—cooking simple meals that have worked for the family before; not taking risks on weeknights. I get the satisfaction of seeing the people I love loving a meal and eating together. Plus, my kids are now old enough to clean up.

So, why do I write cookbooks? I do it because I think there are a lot of people out there who like to hear from a person who speaks their language: those who sometimes cook just for the joy of it, but more often cook because they have to put food on the table. So while I am not a trained chef, I have produced thousands of meals since I was ten years old. Maybe they aren't restaurant quality, but my family doesn't want to eat like that every day anyway. I try to offer delicious food that is easily prepared, crowd-pleasing, and unfussy. It's how our family likes to eat, and maybe the way yours does too.

MEALTIME

LASAGNE BOLOGNESE

SERVES **6** • ACTIVE TIME: **1 HOUR** • TOTAL TIME: **1 HOUR 40 MIN**

You'll find this on the dinner table Sunday night at the Seinfeld house.

FOR THE BOLOGNESE SAUCE

- 2 tablespoons extra virgin olive oil, plus more for the dish
- 1 yellow onion, chopped
- 2 teaspoons kosher salt
- 2 celery ribs, finely chopped
- 4 garlic cloves, chopped
- 2 cups chopped button mushrooms (about 8 medium)
- 1½ pounds ground chuck
- ¼ cup tomato paste
- ½ cup dry white wine, such as pinot grigio
- 1 28-ounce can whole tomatoes
- ¼ to ½ teaspoon crushed red pepper flakes
- ¼ teaspoon freshly ground black pepper
- ¼ teaspoon grated nutmeg
- 1 cup whole milk

FOR THE BÉCHAMEL

- 1 tablespoon unsalted butter
- 2 tablespoons all-purpose flour
- 2 cups whole milk
- ¼ teaspoon kosher salt
- ¼ teaspoon grated nutmeg
- ½ cup grated Parmesan cheese, plus more for the top

- 1 9-ounce box no-boil lasagne sheets (15 sheets)

FOR THE BOLOGNESE SAUCE, in a large pot, heat the oil over medium-high heat. Add the onion and ½ teaspoon of the salt and cook, stirring often, for 4 to 5 minutes, until the onion begins to soften. Add the celery, garlic, and mushrooms and cook, stirring often, for 4 to 5 minutes, until tender. Add the meat and cook, crumbling with your spoon, for 5 to 6 minutes, until no longer pink.

Stir in the tomato paste and cook for 1 minute. Add the white wine and cook for 1 minute. Add the tomatoes, red pepper flakes, black pepper, nutmeg, and the remaining 1½ teaspoons salt. Break up the tomatoes with your spoon as they cook. Let the sauce simmer for 15 minutes. Stir in the milk and let simmer for 10 minutes more. Taste and adjust seasoning to your liking.

While the sauce simmers, make your béchamel. In a medium saucepan, melt the butter over medium heat. Add the flour and cook, stirring with a wooden spoon, for 2 minutes. Slowly pour in the milk while whisking constantly to avoid lumps. It will become very thick at first but will smooth out while you continue to whisk and add milk. Add the salt and nutmeg and simmer, stirring, for 3 to 5 minutes, until slightly thickened. Remove from the heat and whisk in the Parmesan.

Preheat the oven (with the oven rack in the middle) to 375°F. Lightly oil a 9 x 13-inch baking dish.

Spread a thin layer of Bolognese sauce over the bottom of the dish. Add a layer of 3 lasagne sheets. Spread 1 cup of Bolognese sauce evenly over the noodles and drizzle ⅓ cup of the béchamel over the sauce. Repeat with 3 more layers. For the final layer, top with the lasagne sheets and the remaining Bolognese sauce and béchamel. Sprinkle a little more Parmesan over the top.

Cover tightly with aluminum foil and bake for 25 minutes, or until the pasta is tender. Remove the foil and bake for 5 minutes more. Let rest for 5 minutes before slicing.

RIGATONI ALLA VODKA

SERVES **4 TO 6** • ACTIVE TIME: **15 MIN** • TOTAL TIME: **25 MIN**

This is a no-regrets meal. You won't regret learning how to make this, because it is the lifesaver of last-minute meals.

2¾ teaspoons kosher salt

1 pound rigatoni

1 tablespoon extra virgin olive oil

3 garlic cloves, chopped

¼ teaspoon crushed red pepper flakes

⅓ cup vodka

1 28-ounce can whole tomatoes

¾ cup heavy cream

½ cup grated Parmesan cheese, plus more for serving

12 fresh basil leaves

FILL A LARGE POT with water 2 inches from the top. Place over high heat and let come to a boil. Add 2 teaspoons of the salt. Cook the pasta according to the package directions (until al dente). Drain in a colander.

Meanwhile, in another large pot, heat the oil over medium-high heat. Add the garlic and red pepper flakes and cook, stirring, until fragrant but not browned, about 30 seconds. Add the vodka and cook until it is nearly evaporated.

Add the tomatoes and the remaining ¾ teaspoon salt and let come to a boil, breaking up the tomatoes with a spoon as they cook. Reduce the heat to medium and simmer for about 10 minutes, or until slightly thickened. Add the cream and simmer for 2 minutes more.

Add the pasta and Parmesan and stir until the pasta is well coated in the sauce and the cheese has melted. Stir in the basil and serve with a little more Parmesan, if you like.

Keep the vodka away from the flame of your stove! It can catch on fire.

PASTA CARBONARA

SERVES **4 TO 6** · ACTIVE TIME: **15 MIN** · TOTAL TIME: **25 MIN**

With so few ingredients, this is where you splurge on quality: organic eggs, good bacon, cheese from Italy—I like Parmigiano-Reggiano or Grana Padano—and lots of freshly ground black pepper.

  2 teaspoons kosher salt, plus more to taste

  1 pound bucatini

  8 thick-cut bacon slices, sliced crosswise into ½-inch-wide pieces

  ½ yellow onion, finely chopped

  4 large egg yolks

  ½ cup grated Parmesan cheese, plus more for serving

  ½ teaspoon freshly ground black pepper, plus more for serving

FILL A LARGE POT with water 2 inches from the top. Place over high heat and let come to a boil. Add 2 teaspoons of the salt. Cook the pasta according to the package directions (until al dente). Scoop out ½ cup of the pasta water before draining the pasta in a colander.

In a medium skillet, cook the bacon over medium heat, stirring often, for about 8 minutes, or until crisp. Add the onion and cook, stirring, for 5 to 6 minutes more, until softened. Remove from the heat.

In a small bowl, whisk together the egg yolks, Parmesan, and pepper. It will be quite thick, so whisk in ¼ cup of the reserved pasta water to make the mixture pourable.

Return the pasta to the pot and stir in the bacon-onion mixture. Now pour in the egg yolk–Parmesan mixture and stir vigorously until the pasta is well coated. Stir in the remaining ¼ cup pasta water, if necessary, to loosen the sauce. Taste for seasoning; you may want to add a pinch of salt. Serve topped with a little more Parmesan and pepper.

SPICY EGGPLANT PASTA

SERVES **4 TO 6** · ACTIVE TIME: **15 MIN** · TOTAL TIME: **1 HOUR 10 MIN**

Simply slice, roast, and toss, and your vegetarians (and non) will be thrilled.

1 large eggplant
1 pint cherry or grape tomatoes
4 garlic cloves, smashed and peeled
⅓ cup extra virgin olive oil
2¾ teaspoons kosher salt, plus more to taste
¼ teaspoon freshly ground black pepper
¼ teaspoon crushed red pepper flakes
1 pound penne
8 ounces fresh mozzarella cheese, cut into ½-inch pieces
16 fresh basil leaves, torn
¼ cup grated Parmesan cheese

PREHEAT THE OVEN (with the oven rack in the middle) to 400°F.

Cut the eggplant into 1-inch pieces and put in a large baking dish. Add the tomatoes, garlic, oil, ¾ teaspoon of the salt, the black pepper, and the red pepper flakes. Toss together to evenly coat with the oil. Roast for 50 to 60 minutes, stirring halfway through, until the eggplant is very tender.

With about 25 minutes left to roast the eggplant, fill a large pot with water 2 inches from the top. Place over high heat and let come to a boil. Add the remaining 2 teaspoons salt. Cook the pasta according to the package directions (until al dente). Drain in a colander.

Return the pasta to the pot and add the roasted eggplant mixture. Stir together. Add the mozzarella and basil and give a quick stir. Taste for seasoning; you may have to add a pinch of salt. Serve topped with Parmesan.

PASTA *with* RICOTTA, ARUGULA, *and* LEMON

SERVES **4 TO 6** • ACTIVE TIME: **15 MIN** • TOTAL TIME: **25 MIN**

Spring-y, light, and fresh, served with a crisp white wine, this dish will mentally transport you to Italy.

2¾ teaspoons kosher salt

1 pound spaghetti

⅓ cup extra virgin olive oil

6 garlic cloves, sliced

4 cups arugula, stems trimmed

¼ teaspoon freshly ground black pepper

¼ teaspoon crushed red pepper flakes

1 cup ricotta cheese

¼ cup grated Parmesan cheese

Grated zest of 1 lemon

FILL A LARGE POT with water 2 inches from the top. Place over high heat and let come to a boil. Add 2 teaspoons of the salt. Cook the pasta according to the package directions (until al dente). Drain the pasta in a colander.

Return the pasta pot to medium heat. Add the oil and garlic and cook, stirring, for about 2 minutes, or until the garlic is golden brown.

Add the pasta and toss it in the garlic oil. Add the arugula and stir until wilted. Sprinkle with black pepper, red pepper flakes, and the remaining ¾ teaspoon salt. Divide among bowls and add a dollop of ricotta to each. Top with the Parmesan and lemon zest.

Fresh baby spinach can easily be swapped for the arugula.

CREAMY MUSHROOM PASTA

SERVES **4 TO 6** • ACTIVE TIME: **30 MIN** • TOTAL TIME: **30 MIN**

For all you mushroom lovers out there, I can't stress this one enough. "This bowl's for you."

- 2¾ teaspoons kosher salt
- 1 pound penne
- ½ pound shiitake mushrooms
- ¾ pound button or cremini mushrooms
- ¼ cup (½ stick) unsalted butter
- 2 garlic cloves, chopped
- ¼ teaspoon freshly ground black pepper, plus more for serving
- ½ cup dry white wine, such as pinot grigio
- ¾ cup heavy cream
- ½ cup grated Parmesan cheese, plus more for serving
- ¼ cup chopped fresh flat-leaf parsley
- 1 lemon

FILL A LARGE POT with water 2 inches from the top. Place over high heat and let come to a boil. Add 2 teaspoons of the salt. Cook the pasta according to the package directions (until al dente). Drain in a colander.

Meanwhile, use a damp paper towel to wipe away any dirt from the mushrooms. For the shiitakes, remove the stems and discard. Slice the caps. For the button mushrooms, trim the dirty bottoms of the stems, then thinly slice the mushrooms (with stems).

In a large skillet, melt the butter over medium-high heat. Add the garlic and cook, stirring, for about 30 seconds, or until fragrant but not browned. Add the mushrooms and stir to coat (I like to use tongs for this). Let cook, undisturbed, for 1 minute. Now cook, stirring occasionally, for about 5 minutes, or until the mushrooms are tender and release their juices. Sprinkle with ½ teaspoon of the remaining salt and the pepper.

Add the white wine to the mushrooms and simmer for 1 minute (you don't want it to completely evaporate). Stir in the cream and simmer for 1 minute more, or until slightly thickened.

Return the pasta to the pot. Pour the mushroom mixture over the pasta and stir to combine. Stir in the Parmesan, parsley, and the remaining ¼ teaspoon salt. Grate the lemon zest right over the pasta and stir again. Serve topped with a little more Parmesan and pepper.

SWEET POTATO RISOTTO

SERVES **4** · ACTIVE TIME: **40 MIN** · TOTAL TIME: **40 MIN**

Cozy, rich, and satisfying. A great late fall meal.

- 4½ cups water or reduced-sodium chicken broth
- 2 tablespoons extra virgin olive oil
- 1 yellow onion, chopped
- 1 teaspoon kosher salt
- 2 garlic cloves, chopped
- 1½ cups Arborio or Carnaroli rice
- 1 pound sweet potatoes (about 2 medium), cut into ½-inch pieces
- 2 teaspoons fresh thyme leaves
- ½ cup dry white wine, such as pinot grigio
- 1 tablespoon unsalted butter
- ½ cup grated Parmesan cheese, plus more for serving
- ¼ cup chopped fresh flat-leaf parsley

Grated zest of 1 lemon

- ¼ teaspoon freshly ground black pepper

Pinch of crushed red pepper flakes (optional)

POUR THE WATER into a medium saucepan and turn the heat on to medium and keep warm.

In a large skillet, heat the oil over medium heat. Add the onion and ½ teaspoon of the salt. Cook, stirring often, for 5 to 6 minutes, until softened. Stir in the garlic and cook for 30 seconds. Stir in the rice. Cook, stirring, for a minute to toast but not brown the rice.

Stir in the sweet potato and thyme. Add the white wine and stir until nearly evaporated.

Add 1 cup of the water to the rice, and while it simmers, stir it occasionally until all of the liquid is absorbed. Continue to stir and add the liquid, 1 cup at a time, letting it absorb before each addition. Before you add the final ½ cup, taste the rice. It should be tender but the center should be just a little chewy. Add the remaining liquid if it's not quite done.

Remove the skillet from the heat and add the butter and Parmesan. Stir energetically. Then stir in the parsley, lemon zest, black pepper, and the remaining ½ teaspoon salt. Serve sprinkled with a little more Parmesan and some red pepper flakes, if you like.

PINE NUT
and PARSLEY
PASTA

SERVES **4 TO 6** · ACTIVE TIME: **25 MIN** · TOTAL TIME: **25 MIN**

This is a great last-minute meal. I keep fresh parsley in my house at all times so I can make this at any moment.

2½   teaspoons kosher salt

1   pound fettuccine

⅓   cup pine nuts

¼   cup (½ stick) unsalted butter

½   cup grated Parmesan cheese, plus more for serving

¼   cup chopped fresh flat-leaf parsley

½   teaspoon freshly ground black pepper

FILL A LARGE POT with water 2 inches from the top. Place over high heat and let come to a boil. Add 2 teaspoons of the salt. Cook the pasta according to the package directions (until al dente). Scoop out ½ cup of the pasta water before draining the pasta in a colander.

Meanwhile, in a small skillet over medium heat, toast the pine nuts for 3 to 5 minutes, tossing occasionally, until golden brown.

Return the pasta pot to medium heat, add the reserved pasta water, and let come to a boil. Add the butter and swirl the pot. Once it's melted, the butter and the pasta water will form a sort of sauce. Add the pasta, turn off the heat, and toss. Add the Parmesan, parsley, pine nuts, pepper, and the remaining ½ teaspoon salt. Toss until nice and creamy. Serve topped with a little more Parmesan.

PASTA AL FORNO *with* BACON BREAD CRUMBS

SERVES **6** · ACTIVE TIME: **20 MIN** · TOTAL TIME: **40 MIN**

Bacon Bread Crumbs. You read that right.

Extra virgin olive oil, for the baking dish

2¾ teaspoons kosher salt

1 pound short pasta, such as ziti or penne

2 bacon slices

¼ cup dried bread crumbs

1 tablespoon fresh thyme leaves

1 cup heavy cream

1½ cups grated aged Cheddar or Gouda cheese

½ cup grated Parmesan cheese, plus more for the top

½ teaspoon freshly ground black pepper

4 cups baby spinach leaves

1 beefsteak tomato

PREHEAT THE OVEN (with the oven rack in the middle) to 400°F. Coat a large baking dish with oil.

Fill a large pot with water 2 inches from the top. Place over high heat and let come to a boil. Add 2 teaspoons of the salt. Cook the pasta for 3 minutes less than the directions call for (you want it very al dente). Drain in a colander and run under cold water to stop the cooking.

Meanwhile, freeze the bacon for 10 minutes (this will make it easier to chop). Thinly slice the bacon crosswise, then chop it into very small pieces. In a small bowl, combine the bacon, bread crumbs, and thyme.

Return the pasta to the pot and stir in the cream, Cheddar, Parmesan, pepper, and the remaining ¾ teaspoon salt. Fold in the spinach.

Pour the pasta into the prepared dish. Using a serrated knife, thinly slice the tomato and layer over the pasta. Sprinkle with the bacon bread crumbs and more Parmesan. Bake for 15 to 20 minutes, until the bread crumbs are golden brown and crispy.

EGGPLANT CUTLETS

SERVES **4** · ACTIVE TIME: **30 MIN** · TOTAL TIME: **35 MIN**

Light but rich and, so, so crunchy. Meaty without the meat. Does that make sense?

½ cup all-purpose flour

3 large eggs

2 cups dried bread crumbs

1¼ teaspoons kosher salt

¼ teaspoon freshly ground black pepper

1 large eggplant (about 1¼ pounds)

¼ cup extra virgin olive oil per batch of eggplant

2 beefsteak tomatoes, sliced

12 ounces fresh mozzarella cheese, sliced

16 fresh basil leaves

¼ cup grated Parmesan cheese

¼ teaspoon crushed red pepper flakes

TO BREAD THE CUTLETS: Place the flour on a plate. In a shallow bowl, beat the eggs with a fork. On a second plate, combine the bread crumbs, salt, and black pepper.

Using a serrated knife, slice off the stem from the eggplant and discard. Trim the bottom. Slice the eggplant into about ⅜-inch-thick rounds (or somewhere between ¼ inch and ½ inch).

Using one hand, dredge each slice in the flour, then in the beaten egg. Let the excess egg drip off before finally dipping into the bread-crumb mixture, pressing to help it adhere. Place on a clean plate.

In a large skillet, heat ¼ cup of the oil over medium heat. Using tongs, add as many cutlets as can fit in a single layer (they should sizzle) and cook for about 3 minutes, or until the undersides are golden brown. Flip the cutlets and cook for 2 to 3 minutes more, until golden brown. Transfer to a paper towel–lined plate. Wipe out the skillet with paper towels and repeat with another ¼ cup oil and the remaining eggplant.

Preheat the oven (with the oven rack in the middle) to 400°F.

Arrange the cutlets in a single layer on a rimmed sheet pan. Top each with a slice of tomato and a slice of mozzarella. Bake for 3 to 5 minutes, until the cheese is melted. Scatter the basil leaves over the tops and sprinkle with Parmesan and red pepper flakes.

BUTTERMILK PANFRIED CHICKEN

SERVES **4** · ACTIVE TIME: **45 MIN** · TOTAL TIME: **45 MIN**

This fried chicken is double crusted for extra crispiness. I like using extra virgin olive oil for my fried chicken, but you can use whatever type of oil you prefer. I also cut the breasts in half so everyone can have both white and dark meat.

1   3½-pound whole chicken, cut into 10 pieces (breasts halved)
1½ teaspoons kosher salt
2   cups all-purpose flour
1   teaspoon garlic powder
½   teaspoon onion powder
¾   teaspoon cayenne pepper
½   teaspoon freshly ground black pepper
1½ cups buttermilk
Extra virgin olive oil, for frying
6   fresh rosemary sprigs
Honey, for serving (optional)

PAT THE CHICKEN dry with paper towels and sprinkle both sides with ½ teaspoon of salt. Let the chicken come to room temperature (about 25 minutes).

In a large bowl, combine the flour, garlic powder, onion powder, cayenne, black pepper, and the remaining 1 teaspoon salt. Pour the buttermilk into a medium bowl.

Dredge the chicken in the flour mixture, making sure each piece is completely coated. Then dip into the buttermilk. Now dredge once more in the flour mixture. Place on a rimmed sheet pan lined with a wire rack.

Fill a large heavy-bottomed, high-sided pot or a Dutch oven with ¾ inch of oil. Place over medium heat (and no higher than medium) and heat the oil until a deep-fry thermometer reads 325°F. If you don't have a thermometer, test the oil by sprinkling in a little flour—it should sizzle immediately.

Carefully add the chicken, skin side down, to the pot without overcrowding (you will most likely have to cook in batches). Fry the chicken, turning occasionally, for 12 to 18 minutes, until golden brown and crisp and cooked through (you can cut into the thickest part of the thigh near the bone to make sure it's no longer pink—the dark meat will take the longest). The oil should maintain rapid but in-control bubbles and the oil temperature should stay around 325°F, so adjust the heat as necessary. Let the chicken drain on a paper towel–lined plate.

Fry the rosemary sprigs in the hot oil for about 30 seconds, or until crisp.

Serve the chicken hot or cold with the fried rosemary. Drizzle with honey, if you like.

Cover your unused burners and nearby countertops with aluminum foil to protect them from splattering oil.

TOMATO and OLIVE ROASTED CHICKEN with GARLIC-THYME MASHED POTATOES

SERVES **4** · ACTIVE TIME: **30 MIN** · TOTAL TIME: **50 MIN**

Cozy and comfy. This one will make everyone feel welcome at your dinner table. Except vegetarians and vegans.

8   skin-on, bone-in chicken thighs (about 3 pounds total)

¾   teaspoon kosher salt

¼   teaspoon freshly ground black pepper

2   teaspoons extra virgin olive oil

1   pint cherry or grape tomatoes, halved

½   cup green olives, such as Castelvetrano

2   tablespoons fresh lemon juice

3   tablespoons chopped fresh flat-leaf parsley

Garlic-Thyme Mashed Potatoes (recipe follows)

PREHEAT THE OVEN (with the oven rack in the middle) to 425°F.

Pat the chicken dry with paper towels. Season both sides with the salt and pepper.

In a large ovenproof skillet, heat the oil over medium-high heat. Add the chicken, skin side down, and cook, undisturbed, for about 10 minutes, or until the skin is golden brown and crisp. Flip the chicken over and add the tomatoes and olives. Transfer to the oven and roast for 20 to 25 minutes, until the chicken is cooked through (you can cut into the thickest part to make sure it's no longer pink).

Serve the chicken over the mashed potatoes. Add the lemon juice and parsley to the skillet and stir to combine with the tomatoes and olives, then spoon over the chicken.

recipe continues

GARLIC-THYME
MASHED POTATOES

Serves 4

2 pounds russet or Yukon gold potatoes, peeled and cut into
    large pieces
½ cup half-and-half, plus more if necessary
¼ cup (½ stick) unsalted butter
4 fresh thyme sprigs
2 garlic cloves, smashed and peeled
¾ teaspoon kosher salt
¼ teaspoon freshly ground black pepper

Put the potatoes in a medium saucepan. Cover with cold water by 2 inches. Place over medium-high heat and let come to a boil. Reduce the heat to medium and simmer for 15 to 18 minutes, until the potatoes can be easily pierced with a paring knife.

Meanwhile, in a small saucepan, combine the half-and-half, butter, thyme, and garlic over medium heat. Let come to a simmer, then turn off the heat and let steep until the potatoes are ready.

Drain the potatoes in a colander and return them to the saucepan. Using a potato masher, mash the potatoes. Use tongs to pluck out the thyme and garlic from the half-and-half mixture, discard, then pour the mixture over the potatoes. Season with the salt and pepper. Mash together until smooth and creamy. If the potatoes are a bit stiff, add a little more half-and-half.

NO GUILT HERE

Over the years, I admit to having been lured by the
promise of eating fads that were going to make me thinner and
help me live longer.

Thus far, all I have to show for these supposedly life-changing programs are dog-eared diet guides and half-empty bottles of vitamin supplements. The main lesson I've learned is that it's best not to try to abide by restrictive laws. I will inevitably rebel. Instead, a moderate, stress-free approach to eating has made my life much more enjoyable—and, it turns out, kept my weight much more stable. When people ask me, "What is your guilty pleasure?" I have no good answer because I try not to associate food with guilt.

I do mostly eat things that are good for me. But I also enjoy things that aren't as good. We are lucky to have an abundance of food in the Western world. How can we feel bad about what we eat when millions of people are starving? Guilt is a luxury. I appreciate that I can make choices, that I can grab something when I want to, that I can put food on the table for my family, that I can eat food that is rich and delicious or light and wholesome. I have come to believe that we should not associate some foods with virtue and others with vice.

Rather, we should respond to what our bodies crave, which sometimes will be foods we consider abstemious and other times will be those we associate with indulgence. I crave both.

To be sure, I am not the kind of person who will eat a bag of chips or a quart of ice cream in one sitting. My husband is. Jerry will eat so much of something that he never wants to see it again (he recently did this with cinnamon sugar pita chips). This is not something I recommend (and it's no fun to witness).

We all know by now that what you put into your body affects how your body functions and how you feel. We also know we have enough stress in our lives; worrying over what to eat doesn't help. If, instead, you listen to your body—eating foods that make you feel great physically and mentally—less healthy choices become less appealing over time. If you don't eat junk food regularly, don't sweat having Doritos or a Ring Ding once in a while. Free yourself of the burdens of dieting and you will find your way toward a balanced diet.

PEACH *and* SRIRACHA CHICKEN OVER COCONUT RICE

SERVES **4** · ACTIVE TIME: **20 MIN** · TOTAL TIME: **50 MIN**

The flavors here will make you forget your woes. Please don't skip the sprinkle of scallions, peanuts, and cilantro at the end.

FOR THE CHICKEN

- 4 skin-on, bone-in, chicken thighs (about 1½ pounds total)
- 4 chicken drumsticks (about 1 pound total)
- ¼ teaspoon kosher salt
- ½ cup peach jam or preserves
- 1 tablespoon grated fresh ginger
- 1 tablespoon Sriracha hot sauce
- 1 tablespoon reduced-sodium soy sauce
- 3 scallions (white and green parts), sliced
- ¼ cup chopped peanuts
- ¼ cup chopped fresh cilantro

FOR THE RICE

- 1 13.5-ounce can coconut milk (about 1¾ cups)
- 1½ cups jasmine rice
- ¼ teaspoon kosher salt

PREHEAT THE OVEN (with the oven rack in the middle) to 425°F.

Pat the chicken dry with paper towels and sprinkle with the salt.

In a large bowl, stir together the jam, ginger, Sriracha, and soy sauce. Add the chicken and toss to coat. Arrange in a large baking dish or rimmed sheet pan and pour any remaining jam mixture over each piece.

Roast for 35 to 40 minutes. After about 20 minutes, if the sauce starts to burn, add about ½ cup of water or just enough to barely cover the bottom of the pan. This will simmer away and give you a delicious sauce in the end. Continue to roast the chicken until cooked through, 15 to 20 minutes more. You can cut into a piece to make sure it's no longer pink.

For the rice, in a medium saucepan, combine the coconut milk, ½ cup water, the rice, and the salt over medium-high heat. Let come to a boil and stir a few times. Reduce the heat to low, cover tightly, and cook for 18 minutes, or until the rice is tender and the liquid is absorbed. Remove from the heat and let stand, covered, for 5 minutes more.

Serve the chicken over the rice and spoon the sauce over the top. Sprinkle with the scallions, peanuts, and cilantro.

CHICKEN PARMESAN

SERVES 8 · ACTIVE TIME: **30 MIN** · TOTAL TIME: **45 MIN**

I'll be making this for the rest of my life if I want to stay married.

4	skinless, boneless chicken breasts (6 to 8 ounces each)
½	cup all-purpose flour
3	large eggs
1½	cups dried bread crumbs
1	teaspoon kosher salt
¼	teaspoon freshly ground black pepper
½	cup extra virgin olive oil, plus more if necessary
2	recipes Marinara Sauce (page 73) or 5 cups of your favorite store-bought marinara
8	ounces fresh mozzarella cheese
½	cup grated Parmesan cheese

PREHEAT THE OVEN (with the oven rack in the middle) to 425°F.

Lay the chicken breasts on a cutting board. Cut off the tenders, if still attached, and set aside. Starting at the thick end of each breast, with your knife parallel to the cutting board, slice through the breast so you cut it in half lengthwise; this will give you 8 thin cutlets total.

Space the cutlets 2 inches apart on the cutting board and cover with plastic wrap. Using a meat pounder or a rolling pin, pound to an even ¼-inch thickness. The thinner the better.

Set up your breading station: Place the flour on a large plate. In a shallow bowl, beat the eggs. On another plate, combine the bread crumbs, salt, and pepper.

Using one hand, dredge each cutlet in the flour, then in the beaten egg. Let the excess egg drip off before finally dipping in the bread-crumb mixture, pressing to help it adhere. Place the cutlets on a clean plate. Repeat with the tenders.

In a large cast-iron or ovenproof skillet, heat ¼ cup of the oil over medium-high heat. Using tongs, add half of the cutlets to the skillet. Cook for 3 to 4 minutes, until the undersides are golden brown. Flip the cutlets and cook for 2 to 3 minutes more, until cooked through. Transfer to a paper towel–lined plate. Heat the remaining ¼ cup oil and cook the remaining cutlets; transfer to the plate. Cook the tenders, adding more oil, if necessary.

Put the cutlets and tenders back in the skillet (or you can put them in a large baking dish). Pour the marinara sauce over the cutlets. Slice the mozzarella and lay over the cutlets, then sprinkle with Parmesan. Bake for about 15 minutes, or until the cheeses are melted. Serve immediately.

MEATBALLS MARINARA

SERVES **6** · ACTIVE TIME: **25 MIN** · TOTAL TIME: **45 MIN**

I like to make extra meatballs and store them in the fridge for snacks, sandwiches, and extra meals during the week. They freeze really well too.

- ¾ cup dried bread crumbs
- ½ cup whole milk
- 3 large eggs
- 1 pound ground chuck
- 1 pound ground pork
- 1 cup grated Parmesan cheese, plus more for serving
- ¼ cup chopped fresh flat-leaf parsley
- 2 garlic cloves, chopped
- 1½ teaspoons kosher salt
- ½ teaspoon freshly ground black pepper
- 3 tablespoons extra virgin olive oil
- 2 recipes Marinara Sauce (page 73) or 5 cups of your favorite store-bought marinara

Salad greens, for serving

PREHEAT THE OVEN (with the oven rack in the middle) to 375°F.

In a small bowl, combine the bread crumbs and milk. Let stand for about 5 minutes, or until softened.

In a large bowl, beat the eggs with a fork. Add the chuck, pork, Parmesan, parsley, garlic, salt, and pepper. Crumble in the soaked bread crumbs. Using your hands, combine the mixture until evenly mixed.

Using wet hands (to help prevent sticking), shape the mixture into balls the size of golf balls (which will give you about 26). Refrigerate for 15 minutes.

In a large, preferably cast-iron, skillet, heat the oil over medium-high heat. In batches, cook the meatballs, turning them, for 6 to 7 minutes, until they are browned on all sides. Alternatively, you can skip the browning in the skillet and brown them in the oven instead: Spray a rimmed sheet pan with nonstick vegetable oil cooking spray. Arrange the meatballs in a single layer and bake for 15 to 20 minutes, until they are lightly browned and hold their shape. Transfer the browned meatballs to a large baking dish.

Pour the Marinara Sauce over the meatballs. Bake for 15 to 20 minutes, until cooked through. Serve with salad greens on the side and a little more Parmesan.

RIB-EYE STEAKS *with* BLUE CHEESE *and* PARSLEY BUTTERS

SERVES **4** · ACTIVE TIME: **20 MIN** · TOTAL TIME: **55 MIN**

These are a birthday or special-occasion meal at our house. You can dress them up with these fancy butters when you feel like it.

FOR THE PARSLEY BUTTER

- ¼ cup (½ stick) unsalted butter, at room temperature
- 1 small shallot, finely chopped
- 1 small garlic clove, finely chopped
- ¼ cup chopped fresh flat-leaf parsley
- ¼ teaspoon kosher salt
- ¼ teaspoon freshly ground black pepper

FOR THE BLUE CHEESE BUTTER

- ¼ cup (½ stick) unsalted butter, at room temperature
- ¼ cup blue cheese (2 ounces)
- 1 tablespoon fresh thyme leaves
- ¼ teaspoon freshly ground black pepper

- 2 bone-in rib-eye steaks (each 1½ pounds and about 1 inch thick)
- 1 teaspoon kosher salt
- ½ teaspoon freshly ground black pepper
- 2 tablespoons extra virgin olive oil

FOR THE PARSLEY BUTTER, stir together the butter, shallot, garlic, parsley, salt, and pepper.

For the blue cheese butter, stir together the butter, blue cheese, thyme, and pepper.

Let the steaks come to room temperature (about 20 minutes). Sprinkle with the salt and pepper.

In a large cast-iron or heavy-bottomed skillet, heat the oil over medium-high heat. Once the skillet is nice and hot, add the steaks and cook for 5 to 7 minutes, until a deep brown crust forms on the undersides. Turn the steaks and cook for 5 to 7 minutes more, until medium-rare and an instant-read thermometer inserted into the center reads 125°F to 130°F. Let rest on a cutting board for 10 minutes. Top with one or both of the compound butters and slice.

RED WINE and SHALLOT BEEF STEW

SERVES **4** • ACTIVE TIME: **40 MIN** • TOTAL TIME: **3 HOURS 30 MIN**

Rainy or snowy Sundays often call for stew. So, cook this one up and let it simmer away as the aromas waft through the house. Throw a side of bread next to the stove, and it's a serve-yourself meal for everyone.

2½	pounds boneless chuck roast, cut into 2-inch cubes
1	teaspoon kosher salt
½	teaspoon freshly ground black pepper
¼	cup all-purpose flour
2	tablespoons extra virgin olive oil, plus more if necessary
2	tablespoons tomato paste
2	cups dry red wine, such as pinot noir or Chianti
1	28-ounce can whole tomatoes
8	shallots
2	dried bay leaves
1	pound medium carrots (about 8), halved crosswise and lengthwise
1½	pounds medium Yukon gold potatoes (about 6), quartered
¼	cup chopped fresh flat-leaf parsley

PREHEAT THE OVEN (with the oven rack in the middle) to 300°F.

Season the meat with the salt and pepper. In a large bowl, toss the meat with the flour, shaking off the excess.

In a large Dutch oven or pot, heat the oil over medium-high heat. Add half of the meat and cook for 10 to 12 minutes, turning occasionally, until a dark brown crust forms. Transfer to a plate. Repeat with the remaining meat, adding more oil as necessary to the pot, and transfer to the plate.

Turn off the heat and add the tomato paste to the pot and stir for 30 seconds to let it cook in the residual heat. Add the red wine, tomatoes, and 1 cup water. Turn the heat on to medium-high and let the mixture come to a boil while breaking up the tomatoes with a spoon. Add the shallots and bay leaves. Return the meat and the accumulated juices back to the pot. Cover tightly and transfer to the oven.

Roast for 2 hours, or until the meat is just tender. Nestle in the carrots and potatoes, cover, and return to the oven for 1 hour more, or until the vegetables are tender and the meat is fork-tender. Remove and discard the bay leaves. Sprinkle with the parsley and serve.

BLUE CHEESE BURGERS *with* CARAMELIZED ONIONS *and* CRISPY ROSEMARY

SERVES **4** · ACTIVE TIME: **25 MIN** · TOTAL TIME: **25 MIN**

This will quickly become your favorite pub burger, made in your own personal pub. A brioche bun is a nice added touch.

3 tablespoons extra virgin olive oil

4 fresh rosemary sprigs

2 medium red onions, thinly sliced into half-moons

1 teaspoon kosher salt

1½ pounds ground chuck

½ teaspoon freshly ground black pepper

4 ounces blue cheese (about 1 cup, crumbled)

4 hamburger buns

8 butter lettuce leaves

IN A LARGE SKILLET, heat the oil over medium heat. Add the rosemary sprigs and fry for about 1 minute, or until the leaves are crispy. Use tongs to pluck the sprigs out of the oil and place on a paper towel. When cool enough to handle, pull the leaves from the sprigs.

Add the onions and ¼ teaspoon of the salt to the skillet and stir to coat. Cover and let cook, undisturbed, for 7 to 8 minutes, until they start to soften. Remove the lid and continue to cook, stirring occasionally, for 7 to 8 minutes more, until softened and caramelized. Remove from the heat and stir in the rosemary leaves.

Preheat the oven (with the oven rack in the middle) to 400°F.

Shape the beef into 4 patties about ¾ inch thick. Sprinkle both sides with the pepper and the remaining ¾ teaspoon salt.

Heat a large skillet, preferably cast-iron, over medium heat. Add the patties and cook for 5 to 6 minutes, until the undersides have a nice dark brown crust. Flip the patties and cook for 5 to 6 minutes more for medium doneness. (Sorry about the splatters!!)

Transfer the burgers to a rimmed sheet pan. Dividing evenly, crumble the blue cheese over each burger. Bake for 2 to 3 minutes, until the cheese melts. Warm your buns at the same time.

Build your burgers with the buns, patties, lettuce, and caramelized onions and rosemary.

SERIOUS CHILI *with* JALAPEÑO CORN BREAD

SERVES **8** · ACTIVE TIME: **40 MIN** · TOTAL TIME: **3 HOURS 40 MIN**

Beef brisket makes this chili seriously delicious.

- 2 pounds beef brisket, cut into 1-inch pieces
- 2 teaspoons kosher salt
- ½ teaspoon freshly ground black pepper
- 2 tablespoons extra virgin olive oil
- 2 yellow onions, chopped
- 4 garlic cloves, chopped
- 2 tablespoons tomato paste
- 2 tablespoons chili powder
- 1 tablespoon ground cumin
- 2 teaspoons chipotle powder
- 1 28-ounce can crushed fire-roasted tomatoes
- 1 12-ounce bottle or can pale ale
- 1 tablespoon dark brown sugar
- 2 teaspoons dried oregano
- ½ teaspoon ground cinnamon
- 3 15-ounce cans kidney beans, drained and rinsed
- 3 bell peppers (any color), cut into 1-inch pieces

Sour cream, chopped red onion, sliced jalapeño pepper, for serving

Jalapeño Corn Bread (recipe follows)

SEASON THE MEAT with 1 teaspoon of the salt and the pepper. In a large Dutch oven or pot, heat 1 tablespoon of the oil over medium-high heat. Add half of the meat and cook for 8 to 10 minutes, until well browned on all sides. Transfer to a plate. Add the remaining 1 tablespoon oil and brown the rest of the meat. Transfer to the plate.

Add the onions to the pot, stir, cover tightly, and cook, stirring occasionally, for 6 to 7 minutes, until softened. Stir in the garlic and cook for 1 minute. Add the tomato paste, chili powder, cumin, and chipotle powder and cook, stirring, for 1 to 2 minutes, until the tomato paste starts to caramelize. Add the tomatoes, beer, brown sugar, oregano, cinnamon, the remaining 1 teaspoon salt, and 1 cup water and let come to a boil.

Add the meat and any accumulated juices back to the pot. Reduce the heat to low, cover tightly, and simmer, stirring occasionally, for about 2½ hours, or until the meat is tender. Stir in the beans and bell peppers and simmer, uncovered, until the bell peppers are tender, about 30 minutes more.

Serve with sour cream, red onion, and jalapeño. And Jalapeño Corn Bread.

recipe continues

JALAPEÑO CORN BREAD

Serves 8

You can also serve this with Quinoa Chili That Is Not Silly (page 66). And why not Red Wine and Shallot Beef Stew (page 199)?

¼ cup (½ stick) unsalted butter
1¼ cups all-purpose flour
1 cup yellow cornmeal (any grind)
⅓ cup sugar
1½ teaspoons baking soda
¾ teaspoon kosher salt
2 large eggs
1½ cups buttermilk
1 jalapeño pepper, seeded and chopped

Preheat the oven (with the oven rack in the middle) to 425°F.

Put the butter in a 9- to 10-inch cast-iron skillet or a 9-inch round cake pan. Place in the oven for a few minutes until the butter melts.

Meanwhile, in a large bowl, whisk together the flour, cornmeal, sugar, baking soda, and salt. In a medium bowl, whisk together the eggs and buttermilk.

Swirl the hot skillet to coat the bottom and sides with the butter, then pour into the buttermilk mixture and whisk. Add the wet ingredients to the dry ingredients and whisk until just combined. Stir in the jalapeño.

Scrape the batter into the hot pan and bake for 18 to 20 minutes, until a toothpick inserted into the center comes out clean. Serve warm.

I like to use a medium-grind cornmeal in my corn bread for a little texture.

SWEET and STICKY PORK RIBS

SERVES **4** • ACTIVE TIME: **15 MIN** • TOTAL TIME: **1 HOUR 30 MIN**

These are a Super Bowl favorite at our house.

- ½ cup reduced-sodium soy sauce
- ¼ cup apricot jam or preserves
- ¼ cup packed dark brown sugar
- 2 tablespoons Sriracha hot sauce
- 1 tablespoon rice vinegar
- 2 tablespoons grated fresh ginger
- 4 garlic cloves, smashed and peeled
- 2 racks baby back ribs (about 4 pounds total), cut into individual ribs (about 26 total)

Ask your butcher to cut the rack of ribs into individual ribs for you.

IN A SMALL BOWL, combine the soy sauce, jam, brown sugar, Sriracha, vinegar, ginger, and garlic.

Put the ribs in a large ziptop plastic bag. Add the soy sauce marinade, squeeze out the air, and tightly seal. Let marinate in the refrigerator for at least 1 hour or overnight.

Preheat the oven (with the oven rack in the middle) to 350°F.

Arrange the ribs in a single layer on a rimmed sheet pan. Pour in the marinade. Cover the pan tightly with aluminum foil and bake for 1 hour. Remove the foil and raise the oven temperature to 450°F. Roast for 20 to 30 minutes more, basting and stirring the ribs 2 or 3 times, until the marinade becomes sticky and clings to the ribs.

POTATO-TOPPED MEAT LOAF

SERVES **4** • ACTIVE TIME: **20 MIN** • TOTAL TIME: **1 HOUR 30 MIN**

This meat loaf is super-kid-friendly but sophisticated enough for adults.

Nonstick vegetable oil cooking spray
⅓ cup dried bread crumbs
⅓ cup whole milk
1 large egg
1½ pounds ground chuck
1 small yellow onion, chopped
¼ cup chopped fresh flat-leaf parsley, plus more, for serving
1 cup grated sharp Cheddar cheese (4 ounces)
¼ cup plus 2 tablespoons ketchup
¾ teaspoon kosher salt
¼ teaspoon freshly ground black pepper
1 medium Yukon gold potato (about 6 ounces)
2 teaspoons extra virgin olive oil

PREHEAT THE OVEN (with the oven rack in the middle) to 400°F. Coat the inside of an 8½ x 4½-inch loaf pan with cooking spray.

In a small bowl, combine the bread crumbs and milk and let soak for 5 minutes until softened.

Crack the egg into a large bowl and beat with a fork. Add the meat, onion, parsley, Cheddar, ¼ cup of the ketchup, the salt, and pepper, and crumble in the softened bread crumbs. Using your hands, gently mix until well combined.

Add the meat mixture to the prepared pan, gently forming it to the shape of the pan. In a small bowl, combine the remaining 2 tablespoons ketchup with 2 tablespoons water. Spread over the top.

Slice the potato as thinly as you possibly can. Layer over the top of the meat loaf and brush with the oil. Place the pan on a rimmed sheet pan.

Bake the meat loaf for about 1 hour, or until the potatoes are tender and an instant-read thermometer reads 160°F when inserted into the center. Sprinkle the top with a little parsley. Let rest for 10 minutes before slicing.

PORK CHOPS
with TARRAGON-MUSTARD SAUCE

SERVES **4** · ACTIVE TIME: **20 MIN** · TOTAL TIME: **20 MIN**

The simplest of meals. The easy sauce makes you seem like a pro.

- 4 boneless pork loin chops (each 6 to 8 ounces and about 1 inch thick)
- ½ teaspoon kosher salt
- ¼ teaspoon freshly ground black pepper
- 2 teaspoons extra virgin olive oil
- ¾ cup reduced-sodium chicken broth or water
- 3 tablespoons Dijon mustard
- ¼ cup heavy cream
- 1 small bunch fresh tarragon

SEASON THE PORK with the salt and pepper. Let come up to room temperature (about 15 minutes).

In a large skillet, heat the oil over medium-high heat. Using tongs, add the pork (you should hear a gratifying sizzle). Cook for 5 to 6 minutes, until the undersides are golden brown. Flip the pork (the chops should release easily from the pan) and continue to cook for 5 to 6 minutes more, until an instant-read thermometer inserted into the center through the side reads 145°F (it's okay if they are slightly pink in the middle). Use your tongs to hold each chop on its side to sear the fat. Transfer the pork to a plate and discard the fat from the skillet.

Return the skillet to medium heat, add the chicken broth, and simmer for 30 seconds. Whisk in the mustard and cream and let come to a boil. Simmer for 1 to 3 minutes, until slightly thickened. Add any of the juices that have accumulated on the plate of pork back into the sauce.

Return the pork chops to the skillet and cover with sauce. Use scissors to snip the tarragon (about 2 tablespoons) over the pork chops.

PULLED BBQ CHICKEN SANDWICHES *with* COLESLAW

SERVES **8** · ACTIVE TIME: **40 MIN** · TOTAL TIME: **1 HOUR 15 MIN**

I can sell anything on a hamburger bun. In one bite, these sell themselves.

FOR THE CHICKEN

  3 pounds skinless, boneless chicken thighs
  1 tablespoon extra virgin olive oil
  1½ teaspoons chili powder
  1½ teaspoons ground cumin
  ¾ teaspoon kosher salt

FOR THE BBQ SAUCE

  1½ cups ketchup
  ½ cup cider vinegar
  ¼ cup packed dark brown sugar
  1 tablespoon unsulfured molasses
  1 tablespoon Worcestershire sauce
  1 tablespoon dry mustard powder
  1¾ teaspoons freshly ground black pepper
  ¼ to ½ teaspoon cayenne pepper
  1½ teaspoons kosher salt
  1½ teaspoons all natural liquid smoke (optional)

  Coleslaw (recipe follows)
  8 soft sandwich rolls

PREHEAT THE OVEN (with the oven rack in the middle) to 350°F.

Pat the chicken dry with paper towels. Trim away any extraneous fat. Put the chicken in a large baking dish. Drizzle with the oil. In a small bowl, combine the chili powder, cumin, and salt. Sprinkle over both sides of the chicken and rub to coat completely. Cover the dish tightly with foil. Bake for about 1 hour, or until the chicken is cooked through and pulls apart easily.

For the BBQ sauce, in a medium saucepan over medium-high heat, whisk together the ketchup, vinegar, brown sugar, molasses, Worcestershire sauce, mustard powder, black pepper, cayenne, salt, liquid smoke, if using, and ¼ cup plus 2 tablespoons water. Let come to a boil, then reduce the heat to low and simmer for 15 minutes to let the flavors come together.

Use two forks to shred the chicken into a medium bowl. Stir in as much or as little BBQ sauce as you like (refrigerate the rest; it will last for a month in the fridge). Spoon the chicken and Coleslaw into the rolls.

recipe continues

COLESLAW

Serves 8

¼ cup mayonnaise
3 tablespoons fresh lemon juice
1 tablespoon dark brown sugar
½ teaspoon kosher salt
¼ teaspoon freshly ground black pepper
½ head of green cabbage, shredded (about 6 cups)
1 cup grated carrot (about 2 medium)
2 scallions (white and light-green parts), sliced

In a large bowl, whisk together the mayonnaise, lemon juice, brown sugar, salt, and pepper. Add the cabbage, carrot, and scallions. Toss well.

GRANNY

*Everyone who knows me knows my grandmother
was my world. She shaped me in important ways, even after her
death at the age of ninety-nine.*

Granny believed food should be both nourishing and enjoyable. She looked forward to three solid meals each day. Breakfast—when you were supposed to quietly read *The New York Times* cover to cover—usually started with orange juice followed by scrambled eggs, toast, and coffee. Sometimes it involved an English muffin, butter, and jam.

Lunch was almost always a tomato and mayonnaise sandwich on white bread, a piece of fruit, and a glass of water. Dinner was more varied but always included meat, potato or pasta, a vegetable, and a salad. As a divorced single working mother, Granny cooked every night for my mom. Then she cooked for the man who became my grandpa. When he died, she cooked for herself until she couldn't walk anymore.

Granny loved to entertain. As much as she loved her many friends, she had little patience for those who became consumed by fad diets or what she considered peculiar food restrictions and would suggest to them that they simply eat all foods in moderation. She struggled to accommodate guests who would not eat red meat or chicken. She scorned those who claimed they could not eat dairy products.

Granny seemed to believe that people who said they could not tolerate certain foods were self-indulgent and she resented altering her menu for them. She even viewed her husband's life-threatening allergy to nuts with suspicion. Granny was big with the eye roll when it came to food issues. In her later years she was particularly shocked by the way parents catered to their children's food preferences, believing that children should eat whatever the rest of the family is eating.

One of the most important parts of Granny's day—the time she perhaps looked forward to the most—was the Cocktail Hour. A sherry, martini, or bourbon on the rocks—at 6:00 P.M. each day she would have a glass in her hand and classical music or NPR's *All Things Considered* on the radio. When my grandfather came into her life, the ritual began to include cheese, crackers, potato chips, olives, and other bites. There were always friends dropping in during Cocktail Hour, which could then expand to two or three hours. Sometimes, my grandparents would have to be reminded to eat dinner, or that perhaps the rest of us wanted to eat dinner too. They were happy to just drink, nosh, and chat all night long. These evenings instilled in me a love of gregarious company, great food, and good booze.

SHRIMP SCAMPI

SERVES **4** • ACTIVE TIME: **20 MIN** • TOTAL TIME: **20 MIN**

This is an A+ meal. Buy the shrimp already deveined. It's worth the money.

- 6 tablespoons (¾ stick) unsalted butter
- 4 garlic cloves, finely chopped
- ½ cup dry white wine, such as pinot grigio
- 1 pint cherry or grape tomatoes, quartered
- ½ teaspoon kosher salt
- ¼ teaspoon freshly ground black pepper
- ⅛ teaspoon crushed red pepper flakes
- 1¼ pounds peeled and deveined large shrimp
- ¼ cup chopped fresh flat-leaf parsley
- 3 cups cooked white or jasmine rice (see page 157)

IN A LARGE SKILLET, melt the butter over medium heat. Add the garlic and cook for 30 seconds (you do not want it to brown). Add the white wine, tomatoes, salt, black pepper, and red pepper flakes and simmer for 2 to 3 minutes, until the tomatoes start to soften.

Add the shrimp and simmer gently for 4 to 5 minutes, turning the shrimp halfway through, until opaque throughout (you can cut into the thickest part to make sure). Stir in the parsley. Serve over the rice.

CRISPY FISH *with* TARTAR SAUCE

SERVES **4** • ACTIVE TIME: **25 MIN** • TOTAL TIME: **25 MIN**

This classic turned my family into fish lovers.

FOR THE TARTAR SAUCE

- ½ cup chopped dill pickles or cornichons
- 2 tablespoons chopped capers
- 1 tablespoon chopped fresh tarragon
- ½ cup mayonnaise

Few dashes of hot sauce, such as Tabasco

FOR THE FISH

- ¼ cup all-purpose flour
- 1 teaspoon paprika
- 1 large egg
- ¾ cup dried bread crumbs
- 4 sole fillets (about 4 ounces each)
- ¼ teaspoon kosher salt
- ⅛ teaspoon freshly ground black pepper

Grated zest of 1 lemon, zested lemon reserved

- 6 tablespoons extra virgin olive oil

TO MAKE THE TARTAR SAUCE, in a small bowl, combine the pickles, capers, tarragon, mayonnaise, and hot sauce. Refrigerate.

Set up your breading station: On a large plate, combine the flour and paprika. Crack the egg into a shallow bowl and beat with a fork. Put the bread crumbs on another large plate. Line a rimmed sheet pan with parchment paper and place nearby.

Season each fillet with the salt and pepper and sprinkle with the lemon zest. Lightly coat a fillet with flour. Then dip both sides into the egg and shake off the excess before dredging in the bread crumbs. Place on the sheet pan and repeat with the other fillets.

In a large skillet, heat 3 tablespoons of the oil over medium-high heat. Add 2 of the fillets and cook for 2 to 3 minutes per side, until golden, crisp, and cooked through. Transfer to a paper towel–lined plate. Wipe out the skillet with a paper towel and repeat with the remaining 3 tablespoons oil and 2 fillets.

Cut the zested lemon into wedges and serve alongside the fish and tartar sauce.

CLAMS and CHORIZO with HERB AÏOLI TOASTS

SERVES **4** • ACTIVE TIME: **35 MIN** • TOTAL TIME: **35 MIN**

Aïoli (inspired by Shep, the aïoli lover in our family) is a gorgeous complement to the spicy chorizo.

FOR THE HERB AÏOLI

- 1 small garlic clove
- 1 large egg yolk
- 1 teaspoon fresh lemon juice
- ¾ cup extra virgin olive oil
- ½ teaspoon kosher salt
- 1 tablespoon chopped fresh flat-leaf parsley

FOR THE TOASTS

- 8 ½-inch-thick slices baguette
- 2 tablespoons extra virgin olive oil

FOR THE CLAMS

- 48 littleneck clams
- 2 tablespoons extra virgin olive oil
- 1 yellow onion, chopped
- 2 garlic cloves, sliced
- 1 6-inch piece Spanish (dry-cured) chorizo (about 3 ounces)
- 1 cup dry white wine, such as pinot grigio
- ¼ cup chopped fresh flat-leaf parsley

FOR THE AÏOLI, finely chop the garlic into a paste. Put it in a medium bowl and add the egg yolk and lemon juice. Whisk together. Then, very slowly at first, whisk in the oil a little at a time. As the mixture begins to thicken, you can start to pour the oil in a steady stream while continually whisking. If the aïoli is a little thick at the end, whisk in a few drops of water. Stir in the salt and parsley.

For the toasts, preheat the broiler (with the oven rack about 4 inches from the top).

Brush both sides of the baguette slices with the oil. Broil for 1 to 2 minutes per side, until toasted. Set aside.

To make the clams, put a colander in a large bowl in the sink. Add the clams and fill the bowl with cold water. Let the clams soak a few minutes, then rub with your fingers to dislodge any dirt; drain. Throw away any clams that remain open.

In a large pot, heat the oil over medium heat. Add the onion and garlic and stir to coat. Cook, stirring often, for 6 to 7 minutes, until the onion is tender and light golden brown.

Cut the chorizo in half lengthwise, then slice it crosswise into thin half-moons. Add to the pot and cook for 2 minutes, or until the chorizo starts to crisp at the edges. Add the white wine. Stir in the clams, cover tightly, and cook for 6 to 8 minutes, until they open. Discard any clams that won't open.

Divide the clams, chorizo, and broth into bowls and sprinkle with the parsley. Serve with the toasts and aïoli.

MEXICAN BEER-BATTERED FISH TACOS *with* CHIPOTLE CREAM

SERVES **4** · ACTIVE TIME: **25 MIN** · TOTAL TIME: **25 MIN**

I know what you're thinking: there's no way I would make these. You have to trust me here. These are so easy and devastatingly delicious. You will churn out a restaurant-quality meal from your own sweet kitchen in minutes.

FOR THE CHIPOTLE CREAM

- 1 cup sour cream
- 1 teaspoon chipotle powder
- Pinch plus ¾ teaspoon of kosher salt

FOR THE TACOS

- 8 ounces flaky white fish fillet, such as hake or cod (about 1 inch thick and 3 inches wide)
- 1 cup all-purpose flour
- 1 teaspoon baking powder
- ½ cup plus 3 tablespoons Mexican beer, such as Negra Modelo
- 8 corn tortillas
- Extra virgin olive oil, for frying
- 3 cups finely shredded cabbage (purple and green)
- ½ cup fresh cilantro leaves
- 2 limes, cut into wedges

TO MAKE THE CHIPOTLE CREAM, in a small bowl, stir together the sour cream, chipotle powder, and a pinch of salt. Refrigerate.

For the tacos, slice the fish into about ½-inch-thick pieces (you should get 8 pieces).

In a medium bowl, whisk together the flour, baking powder, and the remaining ¾ teaspoon salt. Whisk in the beer. The batter should be smooth and thick enough to cling to the fish. If it's too thick and clumpy, add another tablespoon of beer.

Warm the tortillas: Heat a large dry skillet or cast-iron skillet over medium-high heat. Add as many tortillas as will fit in a single layer. Cook for 1 to 2 minutes per side, until speckled with toasty brown spots but still pliable. Keep warm in a clean dish towel. Repeat with the remaining tortillas.

In a medium skillet, heat ¼ inch of oil over medium heat. Test the oil with a drop of batter to make sure it's nice and hot. If it sizzles, you're ready. Dip a piece of fish into the batter, shake off excess, and add to the oil. Repeat with the rest of the fish. Cook for 2 to 3 minutes, turning halfway through, until golden brown and crisp. Transfer to a paper towel–lined plate.

Fill the tortillas with the cabbage, fish, chipotle cream, and cilantro. Serve with the lime wedges.

PEPPER JACK *and* ZUCCHINI QUESADILLAS

SERVES **4** · ACTIVE TIME: **15 MIN** · TOTAL TIME: **15 MIN**

People love quesadillas. This one was a top hit on my Instagram, so I am including it for you here.

1 large zucchini

4 8-inch flour tortillas

2 cups grated Monterey Jack or pepper Jack cheese

2 tablespoons (¼ stick) unsalted butter

2 cups wild arugula

2 avocados, diced

¼ cup roasted pepitas (pumpkin seeds)

2 tablespoons extra virgin olive oil

1 lemon, cut in half

Pinch of kosher salt

Pinch of freshly ground black pepper

USING THE LARGE HOLES on a box grater, grate the zucchini.

Lay the tortillas flat and divide the Jack cheese and zucchini over one half of each. Fold in half.

In a large skillet, melt 1 tablespoon of the butter over medium heat. Swirl the skillet to coat the bottom with butter. Add 2 of the filled tortillas. Cook for about 2 minutes, or until the undersides are golden brown. Flip the tortillas and cook for about 2 minutes more, or until the cheese is melted and the undersides are golden brown. Transfer to a cutting board. Repeat with the remaining filled tortillas and butter. Slice into triangles and divide among plates.

Divide the arugula and avocado and place alongside the quesadillas. Sprinkle with the pepitas. Give each salad a drizzle of oil, a squeeze of lemon, and a sprinkle of salt and pepper.

GREEN ENCHILADAS

SERVES **4 TO 6** • ACTIVE TIME: **1 HOUR 15 MIN** • TOTAL TIME: **1 HOUR 35 MIN**

Making enchiladas takes time, but it's time well spent. You can add shredded poached or roasted chicken to the mix if you feel the need.

FOR THE FILLING

- 2 tablespoons plus ⅓ cup extra virgin olive oil
- 1 red onion, chopped, plus slices, for serving
- 3 medium zucchini (about 1½ pounds), quartered lengthwise and sliced into ¼-inch-thick pieces
- 4 ounces shiitake mushrooms, stems discarded, caps thinly sliced
- 1 cup fresh corn kernels (about 2 ears)
- 2 teaspoons kosher salt
- 2 cups grated Monterey or pepper Jack cheese (8 ounces), plus more for sprinkling

FOR THE SAUCE

- 4 poblano peppers
- 1 cup tightly packed fresh cilantro leaves, plus sprigs, for serving
- 1½ cups heavy cream
- 12 corn tortillas

FOR THE FILLING, in a large skillet, heat 2 tablespoons of the oil over medium-high heat. Add the red onion and cook, stirring often, for about 3 minutes, or until beginning to soften. Add the zucchini and cook, stirring often, for 4 to 5 minutes, until just tender. Add the mushrooms and cook for about 2 minutes, or until tender. Remove from the heat and stir in the corn and 1 teaspoon of the salt. Transfer to a large bowl to cool. Stir in the cheese.

For the sauce, roast the peppers over a high flame on your gas burner, turning often, until the skin is charred on all sides. Alternatively, you can broil the peppers until charred. Put the charred peppers in a bowl, cover, and let steam for about 15 minutes, or until cool enough to handle. Rub off the skin and discard the cores and seeds. Put the peppers, cilantro, and 2 tablespoons water in a blender and blend until smooth. Add the cream and the remaining 1 teaspoon salt. Pulse a few times to combine (don't overblend—it will turn into whipped cream!).

For the tortillas, line a rimmed sheet pan with paper towels. In a small skillet, heat the remaining ⅓ cup oil over medium heat. Cook the tortillas for 15 seconds per side and let drain on the paper towels. (This will make them more pliable and prevent cracking.)

Preheat the oven (with the oven rack in the middle) to 400°F.

Spread a thin layer of the sauce over the bottom of a 9 x 13-inch baking dish.

Fill each tortilla with about ⅓ cup of the filling, roll up, and place, seam side down, in the baking dish. Pour the sauce over the enchiladas and sprinkle with a little more cheese. Bake for about 20 minutes, or until the sauce bubbles. Serve topped with cilantro sprigs and sliced red onion.

CORN CHOWDER *with* BACON

SERVES **4** • ACTIVE TIME: **35 MIN** • TOTAL TIME: **50 MIN**

I love to eat this soup in the summer when corn is at its peak. I shave it right off the cob and into the pot.

4 bacon slices, cut crosswise into ½-inch pieces

1 yellow onion, chopped

1 tablespoon all-purpose flour

3 cups whole milk

1 cup half-and-half

1 pound red potatoes, unpeeled, cut into ½-inch pieces

3 cups fresh or frozen corn kernels (about 4 ears)

2 teaspoons fresh thyme leaves

1½ teaspoons kosher salt, plus more to taste

¼ teaspoon freshly ground black pepper

⅛ teaspoon cayenne pepper

IN A LARGE POT, cook the bacon over medium heat, stirring often, for 6 to 8 minutes, until crisp. Use tongs to transfer the bacon to a paper towel–lined plate.

Add the onion to the pot and cook, stirring often, for 6 to 7 minutes, until softened. Add the flour and, using a wooden spoon, stir for 1 minute. Stir in the milk and half-and-half. Add the potatoes, corn, thyme, salt, black pepper, and cayenne and let come to a boil. Reduce the heat to medium-low and simmer for about 15 minutes, or until the potatoes are tender. Stir in the bacon. Taste for salt; you may want to add a little more.

BLUE CHEESE SALAD *with* GRAPES *and* WALNUTS

SERVES **4** · ACTIVE TIME: **15 MIN** · TOTAL TIME: **15 MIN**

I love this salad. Grapes are an unexpected yet welcome guest to this party.

FOR THE SALAD

½ cup walnuts

1 head of romaine lettuce

1 cup red grapes, halved

FOR THE VINAIGRETTE

1 teaspoon Dijon mustard

1 teaspoon honey

2 tablespoons white wine vinegar

3 tablespoons extra virgin olive oil

¼ teaspoon kosher salt

¼ teaspoon freshly ground black pepper

1 small shallot, thinly sliced

½ cup crumbled blue cheese (see note)

PREHEAT THE OVEN (with the oven rack in the middle) to 375°F.

Spread the walnuts on a rimmed sheet pan and bake for 10 to 12 minutes, until fragrant and crisp. When cool enough to handle, coarsely chop them.

Slice the head of romaine lengthwise down the middle, keeping the core intact. Then cut the leaves crosswise into bite-size pieces (you should get about 8 cups). Arrange on a platter with the grapes and walnuts.

To make the vinaigrette: In a small bowl, whisk together the mustard, honey, vinegar, oil, salt, and pepper. Stir in the shallot and fold in the blue cheese. Spoon the vinaigrette over the salad.

Buy a piece of blue cheese and crumble it yourself. It tastes so much better than the pre-crumbled stuff.

SALAD with CRISPY PROSCIUTTO and FRESH MOZZARELLA

SERVES **4** · ACTIVE TIME: **15 MIN** · TOTAL TIME: **15 MIN**

Have you ever tried crispy prosciutto? You'll never be the same again.

- ¼ pound thinly sliced prosciutto
- 8 cups salad greens, such as a mix of arugula, radicchio, and frisée
- 8 ounces fresh mozzarella cheese, cut into bite-size pieces
- ¼ cup fresh flat-leaf parsley leaves
- 2 tablespoons extra virgin olive oil
- 2 tablespoons balsamic vinegar
- ¼ teaspoon kosher salt
- ¼ teaspoon freshly ground black pepper

PREHEAT THE OVEN (with the oven rack in the middle) to 400°F.

Place the prosciutto in a single layer on a rimmed sheet pan. Bake for 10 to 15 minutes (depending on the thickness of your prosciutto), until crisp.

Put the salad greens in a large serving bowl and arrange the mozzarella on top. Scatter the prosciutto chips and parsley over the salad. Drizzle with the oil and balsamic vinegar and sprinkle with the salt and pepper.

GARLIC BREAD

Bread. Butter. Garlic. Salt. Four things I want to be buried with.

2 garlic cloves, finely chopped

6 tablespoons (¾ stick) unsalted butter, at room temperature

Pinch of kosher salt

1 baguette

PREHEAT THE BROILER (with the oven rack about 4 inches from the top).

In a small bowl, combine the garlic, butter, and salt.

Using a serrated knife, cut the baguette crosswise in half. Now slice each piece in half lengthwise. Place on a rimmed sheet pan, crust side up, and slide the pan under the broiler and broil about 1 minute, or until the crust is toasted and crisp. Remove the pan and turn each piece over.

Dividing evenly, spread the butter over each piece of bread. Slide the pan back under the broiler and broil for about 2 minutes, or until golden brown and toasted. Slice and serve immediately.

DESSERT

CHOCOLATE FUDGE CAKE

SERVES **10**   •   ACTIVE TIME: **35 MIN**   •   TOTAL TIME: **1 HOUR (PLUS COOLING TIME)**

The perfect chocolate cake.

FOR THE CAKE

Nonstick vegetable oil cooking spray
¾ cup (1½ sticks) unsalted butter
3 large eggs
½ cup sour cream
2 teaspoons pure vanilla extract
2 cups all-purpose flour
1½ cups granulated sugar
½ cup packed dark brown sugar
¾ cup unsweetened cocoa powder
1½ teaspoons baking soda
1 teaspoon baking powder
1 teaspoon kosher salt

FOR THE FROSTING

1¼ cups bittersweet or semisweet chocolate chips
1 cup heavy cream

PREHEAT THE OVEN (with the oven rack in the middle) to 350°F. Spray two 9-inch round cake pans with cooking spray and line the bottoms with parchment paper.

For the cake, in a small saucepan, combine the butter and 1 cup water over medium heat. Heat until the butter is melted.

In a medium bowl, whisk together the eggs, sour cream, and vanilla.

In a large bowl (or the bowl of a stand mixer), whisk together the flour, granulated sugar, brown sugar, cocoa powder, baking soda, baking powder, and salt. Add the butter mixture. Use an electric mixer on low speed to mix until just combined. On medium speed, mix in the sour cream mixture.

Dividing evenly, scrape the batter into the prepared pans. Bake for 30 to 35 minutes, until a toothpick inserted into the center of the cakes comes out with a few moist crumbs attached. Place the pans on a wire cooling rack and let cool for 25 minutes. Run a paring knife around the edge of each cake to loosen it from the pan. Then invert the cakes onto the rack, remove the parchment, and let cool completely.

For the frosting, put the chocolate chips in a medium bowl. In a small saucepan over medium heat, heat the cream until it is hot. Pour the cream over the chocolate and let stand for 1 minute. Now gently whisk until creamy and smooth.

Scoop out ¾ cup of the chocolate mixture into another bowl and set aside the remaining frosting for now. Let the ¾ cup of the mixture cool, stirring occasionally, for about 1 hour, or until it's spreadable, creamy, and holds its shape.

Place one cake on a serving plate, bottom side up. Spread the top with the frosting in an even layer all the way to the edge. Top with the other cake, bottom side up.

Gently reheat the remaining frosting by filling a medium saucepan with 2 inches of water and placing over medium heat. Let come to a low simmer. Place the bowl of frosting over the water (the bottom of the bowl should not touch the water). Stir until it is melted and pourable. Immediately pour the frosting over the top of the cake. With a metal spatula, quickly spread it to evenly cover the top and let the frosting drip down the sides. Once the frosting is set, slice and serve.

COCONUT RUM CAKE

SERVES **15** • ACTIVE TIME: **30 MIN** • TOTAL TIME: **1 HOUR 30 MIN (PLUS COOLING TIME)**

This is my birthday cake of choice. If anyone's asking.

FOR THE CAKE

Nonstick vegetable oil cooking spray

3 cups all-purpose flour

2 teaspoons baking powder

¼ teaspoon baking soda

1 teaspoon kosher salt

1½ cups (3 sticks) unsalted butter, at room temperature

2½ cups granulated sugar

5 large eggs

2 tablespoons dark rum

1 teaspoon pure vanilla extract

3 cups sweetened flake coconut

1 cup whole milk

1½ cups unsweetened coconut flakes

FOR THE FROSTING

1 cup heavy cream

¼ cup crème fraîche

¼ cup confectioners' sugar

PREHEAT THE OVEN (with the oven rack in the middle) to 350°F. Spray a 9 x 13-inch baking pan with cooking spray.

In a medium bowl, whisk together the flour, baking powder, baking soda, and salt.

In a large bowl (or the bowl of a stand mixer), use an electric mixer on medium-high speed to beat the butter until creamy. Add the granulated sugar and beat for 2 to 3 minutes, until light and fluffy. Scrape down the sides of the bowl with a silicone spatula. Add the eggs, one at a time, beating well after each addition. Beat in the rum and vanilla. Use the spatula to stir in the coconut.

With the mixer on low speed, mix in half of the flour mixture, then pour in all of the milk and mix. Now mix in the remaining flour until just incorporated (do not overmix).

Scrape the batter into the prepared pan and smooth the top. Bake for 50 to 55 minutes, until a toothpick inserted into the center of the cake comes out with a few moist crumbs attached. Place the pan on a wire cooling rack and let cool completely.

Spread the coconut flakes onto a rimmed sheet pan. Bake for 6 to 8 minutes, until golden brown.

For the whipped cream frosting, in a large bowl (or the bowl of a stand mixer), combine the cream, crème fraîche, and confectioners' sugar. Using an electric mixer on medium-high speed, beat until medium peaks form. Spread over the top of the cake and sprinkle on the coconut flakes. Cut into squares and serve.

CREAMIEST CHEESECAKE with GRAHAM CRACKER CRUST

SERVES **10** • ACTIVE TIME: **30 MIN** • TOTAL TIME: **1 HOUR 30 MIN (PLUS COOLING TIME)**

Julian Seinfeld (our middle son) is a cheesecake aficionado, so it became my mission to get it just right. The water bath is a must for creaminess throughout, and the graham cracker crust is non-negotiable.

FOR THE CRUST

Nonstick vegetable oil cooking spray

About 16 graham crackers

1/4 cup sugar

1/2 cup (1 stick) unsalted butter, melted

FOR THE CAKE

3 8-ounce packages cream cheese, at room temperature (see note)

1 cup sugar

4 large eggs. at room temperature

2 large egg yolks, at room temperature

1 teaspoon pure vanilla extract

FOR THE TOPPING

1 1/4 cups sour cream

1/4 cup sugar

1/2 teaspoon pure vanilla extract

PREHEAT THE OVEN (with the oven rack in the middle) to 350°F. Spray a 9-inch springform pan with cooking spray.

For the crust, put the graham crackers in a food processor and pulse until finely ground. Or you can use a ziptop plastic bag and a rolling pin to pulverize the crackers. Measure the crumbs (2 cups) and add them to a medium bowl. Stir in the sugar and the melted butter until well combined. The crumbs should be moist and hold together when pressed against the side of the bowl. Sprinkle an even layer of crumbs over the bottom of the prepared pan to cover. Then spoon the remaining crumbs into the corners. Using a straight-sided measuring cup or glass, and starting from the center, firmly press the crumbs over the bottom of the pan into a thin,

even layer, then into the corners and up the sides (about 1½ inches). Bake for about 10 minutes, or until the edges start to brown. If the crust slides down after baking, use your measuring cup to press it back into shape while it's still hot. Let cool.

To prepare for the water bath, wrap the bottom and up the sides of the springform pan with a triple layer of foil so that no water can seep in. Place the pan in a large roasting pan.

For the cake, in a large bowl (or the bowl of a stand mixer), use an electric mixer on medium speed to beat the cream cheese until smooth and creamy. Beat in the sugar until smooth. Add the whole eggs, one at a time, beating well after each addition and scraping down the sides of the bowl as necessary. Beat in the egg yolks and vanilla. Pour into the prepared crust.

Transfer the roasting pan to the oven and fill with 1 inch of water. Bake the cake for 60 to 63 minutes, until the cake is just set (it will still be a little jiggly in the center).

For the topping, combine the sour cream, sugar, and vanilla. Let sit at room temperature until the cake is ready. Dollop the sour cream mixture a spoonful at a time over the top of the hot cake, then spread in an even layer (the cake is very delicate, so be gentle). Bake for 5 minutes more.

Carefully lift the cake from the water bath and remove the foil. Let the cake cool on a wire cooling rack for 30 minutes. Run a paring knife around the edge of the cake to loosen it from the pan. Refrigerate for at least 6 hours or preferably overnight. Remove the ring and slice.

It's important that the cream cheese is at room temperature when you begin so everything can mix together smoothly and without lumps.

VANILLA CUPCAKES *with* CHOCOLATE FROSTING

MAKES **12 CUPCAKES** • ACTIVE TIME: **30 MIN** • TOTAL TIME: **50 MIN (PLUS COOLING TIME)**

Look no further for your new favorite vanilla cake and cupcake recipe. The chocolate frosting makes it complete.

FOR THE CUPCAKES

- 1⅓   cups all-purpose flour
- ½   teaspoon baking powder
- ¼   teaspoon baking soda
- ½   teaspoon kosher salt
- ½   cup buttermilk
- 1   teaspoon pure vanilla extract
- ½   cup (1 stick) unsalted butter, at room temperature
- ¾   cup plus 2 tablespoons granulated sugar
- 2   large eggs

FOR THE FROSTING

- 1   cup semisweet chocolate chips
- ½   cup (1 stick) unsalted butter, at room temperature
- ½   cup confectioners' sugar
- ½   teaspoon pure vanilla extract

PREHEAT THE OVEN (with the oven rack in the middle) to 350°F. Line a 12-cup muffin pan with paper liners.

For the cupcakes, in a medium bowl, whisk together the flour, baking powder, baking soda, and salt. In a liquid measuring cup, measure the buttermilk, then add the vanilla.

In a large bowl (or the bowl of a stand mixer), use an electric mixer on medium-high speed to beat the butter until creamy. Add the granulated sugar and beat for 2 to 3 minutes, until light and fluffy. Scrape down the sides of the bowl with a silicone spatula. Add the eggs, one at a time, beating well after each addition.

With the mixer on low speed, mix in half of the flour mixture, then pour in all of the buttermilk mixture. Now mix in the remaining flour until just incorporated (do not overmix).

Dividing evenly, spoon the batter into the cups of the prepared pan. Bake for 18 to 20 minutes, until a toothpick inserted into the center of a cupcake comes out with just a few moist crumbs attached. Place the pan on a wire cooling rack and let cool for 5 minutes, then lift the cupcakes out of the pan to cool completely.

For the frosting, fill a medium saucepan with 2 inches of water and place over medium heat. Let come to a low simmer. Put the chocolate in a medium bowl and place over the simmering water (the bottom of the bowl should not touch the water). Stir until melted and smooth. Alternatively, you can melt the chocolate in the microwave—just be sure to do it in small time increments, stirring each time to ensure it doesn't burn. Let cool, stirring every so often, until cool but still pourable.

In a large bowl (or the bowl of a stand mixer), use an electric mixer on medium speed to beat the butter and confectioners' sugar together until fluffy. Reduce the speed to low and slowly add in the chocolate. Mix until fully incorporated. Beat in the vanilla.

Frost the cupcakes with the frosting.

FOR BIRTHDAY CAKE

Double the cupcake recipe. Spray two 9-inch round cake pans with cooking spray and line the bottoms with parchment paper. Divide the batter evenly between the pans. Bake at 350°F for 32 to 35 minutes, until a toothpick inserted into the center of the cakes comes out with just a few moist crumbs attached. Place the pans on a wire cooling rack and let the cakes cool for 25 minutes. Run a paring knife around the edge of each cake, unmold onto the rack, remove the parchment, and let cool completely. Double the frosting recipe. Frost.

CARROT CAKE

SERVES **12** • ACTIVE TIME: **45 MIN** • TOTAL TIME: **1 HOUR 10 MIN (PLUS COOLING TIME)**

Carrot cake is a weakness—or a strength(?)—of mine.

FOR THE CAKE

Nonstick vegetable oil cooking spray

1	cup walnuts
2¾	cups all-purpose flour
2	teaspoons ground cinnamon
1½	teaspoons baking soda
1	teaspoon kosher salt
4	large eggs
1½	cups granulated sugar
½	cup packed dark brown sugar
1½	cups extra virgin olive oil
2	teaspoons pure vanilla extract
3	cups grated carrots (about 6 medium)
1	cup sweetened flake coconut

FOR THE FROSTING

2½	8-ounce packages cream cheese, at room temperature
2½	cups confectioners' sugar
1	teaspoon pure vanilla extract

PREHEAT THE OVEN (with the oven rack in the middle) to 350°F. Spray two 9-inch round cake pans with cooking spray and line the bottoms with parchment paper.

Spread the walnuts onto a rimmed sheet pan and bake for 10 to 12 minutes, until fragrant and crisp. When cool enough to handle, coarsely chop them.

In a medium bowl, whisk together the flour, cinnamon, baking soda, and salt.

In a large bowl, whisk the eggs. Add the granulated sugar and brown sugar and vigorously whisk together for 30 seconds, or until dissolved. Then, slowly drizzle in the oil while you whisk. Whisk in the vanilla.

Add the dry ingredients to the wet ingredients. Whisk together until just combined (do not overmix). Stir in the carrots, coconut, and walnuts.

Dividing evenly, scrape the batter into the prepared pans. Bake for 38 to 42 minutes, until a toothpick inserted into the center of the cakes comes out with just a few moist crumbs attached. Place the pans on a wire cooling rack and let the cakes cool for 25 minutes. Run a paring knife around the edge of each cake to loosen it from the pan. Invert onto the rack, remove the parchment, and let cool completely.

For the frosting, in a large bowl (or the bowl of a stand mixer), use an electric mixer on medium-high speed to beat the cream cheese until creamy. Add the confectioners' sugar and vanilla and beat on medium-low speed at first, then increase the speed to medium and beat until smooth and creamy.

Place one cake on a serving plate, bottom side up. Spread the top with about 1 cup of the frosting in an even layer to the edge. Top with the other cake, bottom side up. Spread about 1 cup of the frosting over the top. Frost the sides with the remaining frosting.

APPLE GALETTE

SERVES **8** • ACTIVE TIME: **35 MIN** • TOTAL TIME: **1 HOUR 25 MIN (PLUS COOLING TIME)**

I hate to be irritating, but I actually keep dough in my freezer so I can always throw one of these in the oven should I suddenly need to make a galette.

FOR THE CRUST

- 2 cups all-purpose flour, plus more for the work surface
- 2 tablespoons sugar, plus more for sprinkling
- ½ teaspoon kosher salt
- 14 tablespoons (1¾ sticks) cold unsalted butter, cut into small pieces

FOR THE FILLING

- 2 pounds apples, such as Granny Smith (about 6)
- ⅔ cup sugar
- 2 tablespoons all-purpose flour
- ⅛ teaspoon ground cinnamon
- 1 tablespoon unsalted butter, cut into small pieces
- 2 tablespoons apricot preserves (optional)

FOR THE CRUST, in a food processor, combine the flour, sugar, and salt. Add the butter and pulse several times in short, quick pulses until the butter pieces are pea-size. Add 4 tablespoons ice water. Pulse a few times just to incorporate the water (you don't want to overmix). The dough should look like moist crumbs and hold together when pinched. If it's a bit dry and doesn't hold together, add another tablespoon ice water and pulse twice.

Pour the dough onto a lightly floured work surface. Use your hands to gently press the dough together into one piece. Knead the dough a few times to bring together, then shape into a 1-inch-thick round disk. Wrap with plastic wrap and refrigerate while you prepare your apples.

Preheat the oven (with the oven rack in the second to lowest position) to 400°F.

For the apple filling, peel and core the apples. Thinly slice them and add to a large bowl. Add the sugar, flour, and cinnamon and toss.

Tear off a sheet of parchment paper that will fit into a rimmed sheet pan. Then place it on a flat work surface and sprinkle with flour. Place the dough in the center and sprinkle it with flour as well. Pressing evenly, roll the dough out into a large ¼-inch-thick circle, occasionally rotating it to help keep its round shape (sprinkle with a little more flour, both on top and underneath, if the dough starts to stick). Slide the parchment and dough onto the sheet pan.

Pour the apples into the center of the dough and spread into an even layer, leaving a 2-inch border around the perimeter. Lift and fold the border over the apples to hold them in, making pleats as you go around. Refrigerate the galette for 10 minutes.

Using your fingertips, brush the crust with cold water. Sprinkle the crust with some sugar (about 1 tablespoon). Dot the apples with the butter. Bake until the apples are tender, the juices are bubbling, and the crust is golden brown, 45 to 50 minutes. Let cool before slicing.

This is optional, but if you like a little shine to your apples, in a small skillet over medium heat, melt the apricot preserves with a tablespoon of water. Brush over the baked apples.

LEMON MACAROON PIE

SERVES **8** · ACTIVE TIME: **30 MIN** · TOTAL TIME: **1 HOUR (PLUS COOLING TIME)**

This is a worthwhile project for that friend who loves lemon and coconut.

FOR THE CRUST

Nonstick vegetable oil cooking spray

2 large egg whites

2½ cups sweetened flake coconut, plus ¼ cup for the top

3 tablespoons granulated sugar

⅛ teaspoon kosher salt

FOR THE FILLING

1 cup granulated sugar

⅓ cup cornstarch

¼ teaspoon kosher salt

2 teaspoons grated lemon zest (from 1 lemon)

⅓ cup fresh lemon juice (about 2 lemons)

4 large egg yolks

2 tablespoons unsalted butter

FOR THE WHIPPED CREAM

1½ cups heavy cream

4 to 5 tablespoons confectioners' sugar

FOR THE MACAROON PIECRUST, preheat the oven (with the oven rack in the middle) to 325°F. Spray a 9-inch pie plate with cooking spray.

In a medium bowl, whisk together the egg whites until foamy. Stir in 2½ cups of the coconut, the granulated sugar, and salt. Using your fingertips, firmly press the mixture over the bottom and up the sides of the pie plate. Bake for 22 to 26 minutes, or until light golden brown around the edges and the bottom is set. Let cool on a wire cooling rack.

Spread the remaining ¼ cup coconut on a small rimmed sheet pan. Bake for about 10 minutes, or until light golden brown. Set aside.

For the filling, in a medium saucepan, whisk together the granulated sugar, cornstarch, and salt. Whisk in ¼ cup water until smooth and without lumps. Then whisk in another 1¼ cups water. Place over medium heat and whisk while the mixture comes to a boil. Continue to whisk until very thick. Remove from the heat. Whisk in the lemon zest and lemon juice.

Put the egg yolks in a small bowl and whisk together. Scoop out ½ cup of the hot mixture and slowly pour it into the egg yolks while whisking. Now whisk the egg mixture back into the saucepan (this helps prevent curdling). Cook, whisking constantly, over medium-low heat for 2 minutes. Remove from the heat and whisk in the butter until melted.

Pour the hot filling into the piecrust and smooth the top. Refrigerate for at least 3 hours or overnight, until chilled and set.

When ready to serve the pie, make the whipped cream: In a large bowl (or the bowl of a stand mixer), combine the cream and confectioners' sugar. Using a whisk by hand or an electric mixer on medium speed, beat until soft peaks form.

Spread the whipped cream over the pie, leaving a 1-inch border of filling. Sprinkle the toasted coconut over the top.

STRAWBERRY SHORTCAKE

SERVES **8** · ACTIVE TIME: **25 MIN** · TOTAL TIME: **40 MIN (PLUS COOLING TIME)**

This one is for Sascha, our firstborn. She would live on this if I "didn't have so many rules."

FOR THE SHORTCAKES

- 2 cups all-purpose flour
- ¼ cup granulated sugar, plus more for the tops
- 1 tablespoon baking powder
- ½ teaspoon kosher salt
- 6 tablespoons (¾ stick) cold unsalted butter, cut into small pieces
- ¾ cup heavy cream, plus more for the tops

FOR THE STRAWBERRIES

- 2 pints strawberries
- 1 tablespoon granulated sugar
- 2 tablespoons Grand Marnier

FOR THE WHIPPED CREAM

- 2 cups heavy cream
- 6 to 7 tablespoons confectioners' sugar

PREHEAT THE OVEN (with the oven rack in the middle) to 425°F. Line a rimmed sheet pan with parchment paper.

For the shortcakes, in a large bowl, whisk together the flour, granulated sugar, baking powder, and salt. Add the butter. Using your fingertips, rub the butter pieces into the flour mixture until combined and the butter is in small, crumbly but still visible pieces. Add ½ cup of the cream and stir gently to combine. Then stir in the remaining ¼ cup cream. The mixture should be moist but not wet, a little shaggy but not solid. Use your hands to gently press the dough together into one piece.

Place the dough on a lightly floured surface and gently knead a few times until it is uniform (you don't want to be overly aggressive with it). Press into a ¾-inch-thick disk. Using a cookie cutter or a glass (about 2 inches in diameter), cut out 7 shortcakes. Reshape the scraps to make the eighth shortcake. For the highest rise, be sure to cut straight down through the dough without twisting the cutter.

Place the shortcakes on the prepared pan. Pour a small amount of cream (about a tablespoon) into a small bowl and use your fingertips to brush the tops of the shortcakes. Sprinkle them with a little granulated sugar. Bake for 12 to 15 minutes, until golden brown. Transfer to a wire cooling rack and let cool.

For the strawberries, hull and slice them and put them in a medium bowl. Toss with the granulated sugar and stir in the Grand Marnier and let marinate for 10 minutes.

For the whipped cream, in a large bowl (or the bowl of a stand mixer), combine the cream and confectioners' sugar. Using a whisk by hand or an electric mixer on medium speed, beat until soft peaks form.

To serve, slice the shortcakes in half horizontally and fill with the strawberries and whipped cream.

ONE-POT MOCHA BROWNIES

MAKES **16 BROWNIES** · ACTIVE TIME: **15 MIN** · TOTAL TIME: **40 MIN (PLUS COOLING TIME)**

These are easy with minimal dish washing. I throw these in the oven last minute before I show up somewhere for dinner. Even if my presence isn't welcome, these brownies always are.

Nonstick vegetable oil cooking spray

- ¾ cup pecans or walnuts
- ½ cup (1 stick) unsalted butter
- 1 cup semisweet chocolate chips
- 1 tablespoon espresso powder
- ¾ cup granulated sugar
- ¼ cup packed dark brown sugar
- 2 large eggs
- 1 teaspoon pure vanilla extract
- ¼ cup all-purpose flour
- ¼ cup unsweetened cocoa powder
- ¼ teaspoon baking soda
- ¼ teaspoon kosher salt

If you want to get really crazy, instead of adding nuts, add chopped peanut butter cups or peppermint patties. If you want to go insane, crush some espresso beans and add those.

PREHEAT THE OVEN (with the oven rack in the middle) to 350°F. Spray an 8 x 8-inch baking pan with cooking spray. Line with an 8-inch-wide strip of parchment paper, leaving an overhang on two sides.

Spread the pecans onto a rimmed sheet pan and bake for 10 to 12 minutes, until fragrant and crisp. When cool enough to handle, coarsely chop them.

In a medium saucepan, melt the butter over medium heat. Remove from the heat and add the chocolate chips and espresso. Let stand for about 2 minutes, then whisk until creamy and smooth. Whisk in the granulated sugar and brown sugar. Whisk in the eggs, one at a time, and the vanilla. Add the flour, cocoa powder, baking soda, and salt and whisk with gusto for a solid 45 seconds, or until the batter is thick and glossy and pulls away from the pan. Fold in the pecans.

Scrape the batter into the prepared pan and spread evenly. Bake for 28 to 30 minutes, until a toothpick inserted into the center of the brownies comes out with more than a few moist crumbs attached (best to underbake than to overbake). Let cool completely in the pan on a wire cooling rack.

Grab the ends of the parchment and lift the brownies out onto a cutting board. Slice into 2-inch squares.

ORANGE-ALMOND CAKE
with ORANGE SYRUP

SERVES **8** · ACTIVE TIME: **20 MIN** · TOTAL TIME: **1 HOUR (PLUS COOLING TIME)**

There is no time of day or time of year when this cake is not absolutely perfect to serve. Your friends will scream for mercy.

FOR THE CAKE

Nonstick vegetable oil cooking spray

3 cups sliced blanched almonds or 3 cups almond meal/flour

1 cup granulated sugar

½ cup (1 stick) unsalted butter, at room temperature

Grated zest of 1 orange

4 large eggs

½ teaspoon pure almond extract

½ teaspoon baking powder

¼ teaspoon kosher salt

FOR THE ORANGE SYRUP

¼ cup fresh orange juice (from 1 orange)

2 tablespoons granulated sugar

FOR THE WHIPPED CREAM

2 cups heavy cream

6 to 7 tablespoons confectioners' sugar

FOR THE CAKE, preheat the oven (with the oven rack in the middle) to 350°F. Spray a 9-inch springform pan with cooking spray.

If using sliced almonds, put them in a food processor with ¼ cup of the sugar and pulse several times until very finely ground.

In a large bowl (or the bowl of a stand mixer), use an electric mixer on medium-high speed to beat the butter until creamy. Add the remaining ¾ cup sugar (or 1 cup if using almond meal) and the orange zest and beat for 2 to 3 minutes, until light and fluffy. Scrape down the sides of the bowl with a silicone spatula. Add the eggs, one at a time, beating well after each addition. Beat in the almond extract.

With the mixer on low speed, mix in the ground almonds or almond meal, baking powder, and salt.

Scrape the batter into the prepared pan and spread evenly. Bake for 35 to 38 minutes, until a toothpick inserted into the center of the cake comes out with a few moist crumbs attached.

For the orange syrup, pour the juice into a small skillet and add the granulated sugar (you can prep this while the cake bakes and let it sit). When the cake comes out of the oven, turn the heat on under the skillet to medium and let the mixture come to a boil. Simmer for 1 to 2 minutes, until the sugar is completely dissolved and the juice has thickened to a syrup. Use a skewer or toothpick to poke several holes in the cake. Drizzle the hot syrup over the hot cake and spread evenly with the back of a spoon.

Let the cake cool for 25 minutes on a wire cooling rack. Run a paring knife around the edge of the cake to loosen it from the pan, then remove the ring. Let cool completely before slicing.

For the whipped cream, in a large bowl (or the bowl of a stand mixer), combine the cream and confectioners' sugar. Using a whisk by hand or an electric mixer on medium speed, beat until soft peaks form. Serve with the cake.

CHOCOLATE-BANANA PUDDING

SERVES **8** · ACTIVE TIME: **20 MIN** · TOTAL TIME: **20 MIN (PLUS COOLING TIME)**

Pudding is funny. Just when you think nothing is happening in the pot . . . a luscious treat materializes right before your eyes.

FOR THE PUDDING

- ¾ cup granulated sugar
- ⅓ cup cornstarch
- ⅓ cup unsweetened cocoa powder, plus more for serving
- ¼ teaspoon kosher salt
- 4 cups whole milk
- 4 large egg yolks
- ½ cup semisweet or bittersweet chocolate chips
- 1 teaspoon pure vanilla extract
- 2 bananas, thinly sliced

FOR THE WHIPPED CREAM

- 1½ cups heavy cream
- ½ tablespoon confectioners' sugar

Do you like the weird "skin" that forms on the top of pudding? Just don't cover the puddings in plastic wrap when you refrigerate them.

IN A MEDIUM SAUCEPAN, whisk together the granulated sugar, cornstarch, cocoa powder, and salt. Whisk in 1 cup of the milk and the egg yolks until smooth. Now whisk in the remaining 3 cups milk.

Place the saucepan over medium heat and stir the mixture constantly for about 10 minutes, or until it starts to thicken. Reduce the heat to low and continue to whisk for 2 to 3 minutes more, until the pudding has thickened and coats the back of a spoon. Remove from the heat and whisk in the chocolate chips and vanilla.

Set out eight 6- to 8-ounce cups or bowls. Scoop ¼ cup of the pudding into each cup. Add a layer of bananas to each, then spoon in the remaining pudding, dividing it evenly. Tightly wrap each pudding with plastic wrap and refrigerate until completely cool.

When you're ready to serve, make the whipped cream. In a large bowl (or the bowl of a stand mixer), combine the cream and the confectioners' sugar. Using a whisk by hand or an electric mixer on medium speed, beat until soft peaks form. Dollop the whipped cream over the puddings and sift some cocoa powder over the tops.

KEY LIME PIE

SERVES **8** • ACTIVE TIME: **30 MIN** • TOTAL TIME: **40 MIN (PLUS COOLING TIME)**

What's better than a macadamia nut? Many macadamia nuts baked into a buttery graham cracker crust that holds Key lime pie filling.

FOR THE CRUST

Nonstick vegetable oil cooking spray

About 10 graham crackers

½ cup macadamia nuts

2 tablespoons granulated sugar

6 tablespoons (¾ stick) unsalted butter, melted

FOR THE FILLING

4 large egg yolks

2 teaspoons grated regular or Key lime zest (from 2 regular limes)

1 14-ounce can sweetened condensed milk

¾ cup fresh regular or Key lime juice (about 6 regular limes)

FOR THE WHIPPED CREAM

2 cups heavy cream

6 to 7 tablespoons confectioners' sugar

PREHEAT THE OVEN (with the oven rack in the middle) to 350°F. Spray a 9-inch pie plate with cooking spray.

For the crust, in a food processor, grind up the graham crackers. Measure them (1¼ cups) and add to a medium bowl. Add the macadamia nuts and granulated sugar to the processor and pulse into very small but still visible pieces. Add to the crumbs and stir in the melted butter.

Spread the mixture evenly into the prepared pie plate, then, using a straight-sided measuring cup, firmly press the crust over the bottom. Use your fingers to press the crumbs up the sides of the plate. Bake for about 10 minutes, or until the edges start to brown. If the crust slides down the sides or bubbles up at the bottom after baking, use your measuring cup to press it back into shape while it's still hot. Let cool.

For the filling, in a large bowl (or the bowl of a stand mixer), use an electric mixer on medium-high speed to beat together the egg yolks and lime zest. Add the sweetened condensed milk and beat for about 3 minutes, or until fluffy. Slowly pour in the lime juice while mixing.

Pour the filling into the prepared crust and bake for about 10 minutes, or until set. Let cool on a wire rack for 25 minutes. Refrigerate for at least 4 hours or overnight, until completely cooled and set.

When you're ready to serve, make the whipped cream. In a large bowl (or bowl of a stand mixer), combine the cream and confectioners' sugar. Using a whisk by hand or an electric mixer on medium speed, beat until soft peaks form. Serve a dollop of whipped cream over each slice of pie.

MERINGUE CAKE *with* RASPBERRY SAUCE

SERVES **8** · ACTIVE TIME: **30 MIN** · TOTAL TIME: **1 HOUR (PLUS COOLING TIME)**

Ewww. Name Drop Alert. Sorry. My friend Mario Batali suggests that one serve the raspberries and cream on the side if you like a little more crunch in your meringue. I like them piled on. Listen to Mario, though. He knows.

FOR THE CAKE

Nonstick vegetable oil cooking spray

4 large eggs

1½ cups walnuts

About 1 matzo cracker

¼ teaspoon kosher salt

1¼ cups granulated sugar

2 teaspoons cornstarch

½ teaspoon pure vanilla extract

FOR THE RASPBERRY SAUCE

2 6-ounce containers raspberries (about 2½ cups)

3 tablespoons granulated sugar

1 tablespoon fresh lemon juice

FOR THE WHIPPED CREAM

2 cups heavy cream

6 to 7 tablespoons confectioners' sugar

PREHEAT THE OVEN (with the oven rack in the middle) to 350°F. Spray a 9-inch springform pan with cooking spray.

For the cake, separate the eggs: Put the whites in the bowl of a stand mixer or a large mixing bowl. Reserve the yolks for another use (like Pasta Carbonara on page 168).

Finely chop the walnuts by hand or use a food processor to do so; measure and put them in a medium bowl. Put the matzo cracker in a food processor and pulse until finely ground. Or you can use a ziptop plastic bag and a rolling pin to grind the matzo. Measure the crumbs (⅓ cup) and add to the bowl. Add the salt as well. Stir to combine.

Using an electric mixer on medium-high speed, beat the egg whites for about 1 minute, or until soft, foamy peaks form. With the mixer still running on medium-high speed, slowly add the granulated sugar. The meringue should be very thick and silky. Beat in the cornstarch. Using a silicone spatula, gently fold in the walnut mixture and vanilla.

recipe continues

Scrape the batter into the prepared pan and smooth the top. Bake for about 40 minutes, or until the top is a very light golden brown and hard to the touch. Let cool for 25 minutes on a wire cooling rack. Run a paring knife around the edge of the cake to loosen it from the pan, then remove the ring. Let cool completely.

For the raspberry sauce, in a small saucepan, combine the raspberries, granulated sugar, and lemon juice over medium-high heat and let come to a boil. Stir once. Reduce the heat to medium and simmer, without stirring (to keep some berries intact), for 6 to 8 minutes, until the sauce starts to thicken (it will thicken more as it cools). Refrigerate until completely cool.

When you are ready to serve the cake, make the whipped cream. In a large bowl (or the bowl of a stand mixer), combine the cream and confectioners' sugar. Using a whisk by hand or an electric mixer on medium speed, beat until soft peaks form.

Transfer the cake to a platter. Spoon the raspberry sauce over the cake and top with the whipped cream.

Cold eggs are easier to separate. But room-temperature eggs whip up with greater volume. Best to separate the eggs when you take them out of the refrigerator. Then cover the whites with plastic wrap and let them stand at room temperature for about 20 minutes before beating.

ACKNOWLEDGMENTS

JOHN KERNICK, photography

MARK SELIGER, cover photography

PAM MORRIS, stylist

SARA QUESSENBERRY, food stylist

LAURA PALESE, art direction and design

ROBIN POGREBIN, editor

RICARDO SOUZA, everything

Special thanks to PAM CANNON
at Random House

INDEX

Page numbers of photos appear in *italics*.

ABOUT *the* AUTHOR

Jessica Seinfeld is the author of three *New York Times* bestselling cookbooks: *Deceptively Delicious, Double Delicious,* and *The Can't Cook Book.* She is the president and founder of the GOOD+ Foundation (formerly Baby Buggy), a nonprofit organization that has donated more than 30 million items to low-income families through their national network of more than 100 antipoverty programs across the United States. She lives in Manhattan with her husband, comedian Jerry Seinfeld, and their three children, two dachshunds, and two cats.

Facebook.com/jessseinfeld
@JessSeinfeld
Instagram.com/JessSeinfeld